W9-BVV-614

AMERICA AND RUSSIA
IN A CHANGING WORLD

*For
Marie*

AMERICA AND RUSSIA
IN A CHANGING WORLD

A Half Century of Personal Observation

W. AVERELL HARRIMAN

INTRODUCTION BY ARTHUR M. SCHLESINGER, JR.

DOUBLEDAY & COMPANY, INC., GARDEN CITY, NEW YORK

WINGATE COLLEGE LIBRARY
WIN... N. C.

1971

Sept 22, 1971

Library of Congress Catalog Card Number 71–138930
Copyright © 1970, 1971 by W. Averell Harriman
All Rights Reserved
Printed in the United States of America
First Edition

INTRODUCTION

Few Americans in the history of the republic have had richer and more varied public careers than Averell Harriman, and few have served their country with such devotion and wisdom. He has lived an exceedingly full life—in another year he will be eighty—and his lifetime has embraced the extraordinary years of America's rise as a world power. No one in this difficult period has played a larger or longer part in American diplomacy; nor has any participant in the diplomatic enterprise, I think, perceived more lucidly the responsibilities and limitations of the world role thrust on the United States. In this book he has distilled the experience of a turbulent age for America and the world.

When Averell Harriman was born in 1891, Benjamin Harrison was President, the Populists were on the march, the automobile had just been invented, the airplane was still a dozen years in the future, and the population of the United States was sixty-four million, considerably less than a third of the population of 1970. As a small boy, Harriman lived through the two McKinley-Bryan campaigns and was suitably alarmed by the specter of the wild man from the West (in later years he came to believe that Bryan was essentially right on the issues of 1896 and 1900). He was seven years old when the Spanish-American war moved America irrevocably into the center of international power politics. He was thirteen when his father, E. H. Harriman, took him to Japan on the first leg of the railroad builder's notable trip to the Far East where he traveled to explore his dream of a round-the-world transportation system. This was in Septem-

51401

ber 1905, just after the Treaty of Portsmouth, and the boy
witnessed the violent anti-American riots in Tokyo; it gave
him a vivid sense of the explosive nature of the Japanese. But
he could not accompany his father on to Port Arthur and
the mainland, because Dr. Endicott Peabody, the rector of
Groton, declined to let him start the autumn term two weeks
late.

Averell Harriman thus grew up in the first American generation to think instinctively of America as a world power. After
Groton, he went on to Yale, and, after Yale, into Union
Pacific, the family business. But it was evidently hard for him
to confine his energies within the three-mile limit. Following
the First World War, he branched into international banking
and investment (and international polo). Convinced that the
Bolshevik Revolution would be one of the significant events
of the century, he became involved in the twenties in a manganese concession in the Soviet Caucasus. It was this, as he
explained in this book, which took him to Moscow in 1926
and led to his meeting with Trotsky—the first of the long
list of Soviet leaders with whom he was to negotiate over
the next forty years. He went back to Russia fifteen years
later as head, with Lord Beaverbrook, of the Anglo-American supply mission three months after the Nazi attack on
the Soviet Union. In 1943 President Roosevelt appointed
him Ambassador to Russia, and he served in Moscow during
the years when wartime collaboration gave way to the mis-
trust and resentment of the cold war. He returned a number of times in subsequent years, most triumphantly when he
negotiated the test ban treaty of 1963. This long record of
concern with Soviet Russia, followed by his role in 1968 as
head of the American delegation in Paris seeking an end to
the Vietnam war, has given him more experience than any

other American in top-level negotiations with the Communist world.

In considering the value of Harriman's testimony today, one must note the remarkable consistency of his view of Communism over the last half century. He has seen the Soviet Union from the start as a society based on and committed to principles fundamentally antithetical to western ideas of democracy and civil freedom. He has also seen it as a nation with a long and anguished history, dedicated to the defense of its borders and the modernization of its economy, combining cruel repression with fervent hope. And he has seen it as a nation subject to the changes wrought by the passage of time, by the progress of technology and affluence, by the firm and unhysterical external containment of its aggressive impulses and by the force, however much controlled and suppressed, of its internal opinion. The words "in a changing world" in the title of this book are vital to Harriman's sense of international affairs.

He has held steadily to these views, I have noted, for a long time; and it is ironical that the same conception of the Soviet Union should have led some to condemn him as warmonger in 1945 and others to criticize him as soft-on-Communism a quarter century later. The fact is, of course, that what had changed was not Harriman's essential diagnosis of the Soviet Union but the times. When he warned from Moscow in 1944 that Soviet and American interests seemed likely to diverge in the postwar world, when he cabled Cordell Hull that we must "oppose them promptly with the greatest of firmness where we see them going wrong," when at San Francisco in 1945 he advocated American resistance to Soviet demands during the founding conference of the United Nations, he was speaking in the context of a time when the war had generated sentimental illusions about the virtuous purposes of the Soviet Union. When he negotiated the test ban treaty in 1963, when he worked to stop the bombing of North Vietnam in 1968, when he argued for a negotiated settlement with North Vietnam in 1969 and 1970, he was affirming the necessity of specific agreements with various elements in the now fragmented Communist world—agreements essential if the planet were to move at all toward peace.

At no time was he a messianic cold warrior, dedicated to the idea of the extirpation of a fixed and unalterably evil Soviet threat. His mind was always fixed on concrete situations, not on abstract theorems. As he cabled Washington when he was calling for a harder American position in early 1945, "I am as you know a most earnest advocate of the closest possible understanding with the Soviet Union so that what I am saying relates only to how best attain such understanding." His thought was, that, since we could not destroy Soviet Communism, we had to work out the practical ways by which two great powers could live together on the same small planet. He believed that this was to be achieved neither by deferring to the Soviet Union nor by crusading against it but rather by the calm, vigilant and rational defense of democratic interests and by the firm determination to seek agreement where agreement would be of mutual advantage.

Moreover, perhaps because he had seen the world change so much in his own lifetime, he expected that it would continue to change in the future, and the Soviet Union along with it. This may be one reason why he has been so much less rigid in his judgments than the generation of younger diplomats and generals who ran so much of American foreign policy in the fifties and sixties and whose ideas were formed and frozen in the early cold war. Thus Harriman was one of the first to understand the impact the rise of national Communism would have on the old stereotype of the monolithic, centralized Communist empire. He has preserved a cordial personal relationship with Tito through the years; in the Mc-Carthy period he vigorously defended Foreign Service officers like John Paton Davies, Jr., who had committed the sin of arguing that the Chinese Communists were not puppets of Moscow; and he scorned those in the American government who kept on babbling mindlessly about "the Sino-Soviet bloc"—a usage which can, incredibly, be found on the lips of high State Department officials as late as 1965, long after the sounds of discord must presumably have impressed themselves on the deafest ears.

Harriman's combination of flexibility and firmness has, among other things, won him the respect of his adversaries. The Communists plainly see him as a tough and candid negotiator, vigorous in the defense of the American interest, patient and resourceful in the pursuit of common ground. When President Kennedy sent him to Moscow for the test ban negotiations, someone from the Soviet embassy remarked to me: "As soon as I heard that Harriman was going, I knew you were serious." In order to convey the quality of Harriman's relationship with Soviet leaders, it may be permissible now to quote some passages from his conversations in Moscow in April 1963 on a mission to induce Chairman Khrushchev to do something about Laos.

Khrushchev said Mr. Harriman was very clever in trying to put such responsibility on him. The international socialist movement is built on the principle of mutual respect for sovereignty.

"No socialist state interferes in the internal affairs of any other. Each state makes and keeps its own agreements, but you, Mr. Harriman, have not kept an agreement you made with me four years ago. You agreed at that time to become my economic adviser and you have not fulfilled your agreement." Mr. Khrushchev and the Governor, in some good humor, reviewed the details of Mr. Khrushchev's employment offer, including a dacha which the Chairman said was still waiting for Harriman to occupy. He said he had given the ground hog found on the premises to his grandchildren. Mr. Harriman then asked about Khrushchev's family and his grandchildren at which point Khrushchev said he now had two greatgrandchildren. Mr. Harriman said that despite the fact that Khrushchev was younger, he was ahead of Harriman on this point because Harriman as yet had no greatgrandchildren and must conclude that his grandchildren were less active than Khrushchev's. Khrushchev said the trouble was they were capitalists and this just proved that the socialist system was out-producing the capitalist system.

Returning to the subject of Laos. . . .

Later Khrushchev said that Harriman, as his economic adviser, should give him some advice. Very well, Harriman replied, he had a serious suggestion to make. Slapping the table, Khrushchev shouted, "Out with it!" Harriman said, "The advice I would give you would be to come to an agreement on the test ban. This would enable you to devote more of your resources to civilian production." At the end of their talks, Khrushchev said, "I and my comrades regard you, Mr. Harriman, with highest esteem. Your work as Ambassador left a deep and favorable impression here. We all agree that we would like to return our relations to the state they were in during the period when you served here. Enormous results would come from this not only for our two nations, but for the whole world."

A statesman, as Burke pointed out long ago, differs from an ideologue: "the latter has only the general view of society;

the former, the statesman, has a number of circumstances to combine with those general ideas, and to take into his consideration. Circumstances are infinite, are infinitely combined, are variable and transient. . . . A statesman, never losing sight of principles, is to be guided by circumstances." In Burke's sense, Harriman is one of the great statesmen of the century and hence a constant exasperation to true believers, doctrinaires and dogmatists, whether New Left historians or old right Vice Presidents.

What makes for effectiveness in statesmanship? As Burke suggests, the first prerequisite is skill as a diagnostician. As a good doctor can identify a patient's disease without necessarily being able to articulate at once every step in the chain of reasoning which led to his conclusion, so a statesman develops an intuitive sense, as through his finger tips, of the balance of political forces and necessities in the situation in which he is involved. The skill is transferable, which is why Harriman, though his primary experience was in the United States and Europe, could at various times guide (or try to guide) American policy so usefully in East Asia, Latin America and Africa.

A second prerequisite is a determination to defend the legitimate interests of one's own state joined with a recognition that other states have legitimate interests too. A third is to take care that the adversary always has room for honorable retreat: never push a man against a closed door. A fourth is a combination of candor and courtesy with toughness: *suaviter in modo, fortiter in re*. A fifth, especially in dealing with the Communists, is patience in the face of hours of stereotyped and boring rhetoric.

Most important of all, perhaps, is a sense of the way the world is going. By themselves the other qualities will never suffice if a man lacks an instinct for the movement of history.

Burke thus emphasized that, while a statesman must be guided by circumstances, he must never lose sight of principles. Though himself in his early years an active and successful capitalist, Harriman had become before the age of forty a liberal and, in his laconic way, an idealist. His remarkable older sister, Mary Harriman Rumsey, who had helped found the Junior League in 1901 as a means of luring society girls into settlement work, had great influence on her younger brother. Speaking of their father in 1933, Mary Rumsey said, "His period was a building age, when competition was the order of the day. Today the need is not for a competitive but a cooperative economic system."

Averell Harriman, while still believing in the virtues of private ownership and initiative, also believed in the vital necessity of social control. He left the Republican Party to support Al Smith for President in 1928 and Franklin Roosevelt in 1933; he served in the National Recovery Administration in the early thirties, was a leading New Dealer in the business community and a well-established traitor to his class. Later he strongly backed the reform policies of Harry S. Truman, John F. Kennedy and Lyndon Johnson and, as a progressive Governor of New York in the nineteen fifties, himself initiated pioneer programs in the war against poverty, in the defense of the consumer, in civil rights, in air pollution and in other areas of social concern.

His dedication to the improvement of American society has been as profound as his concern with the American position in the world; indeed, as this book makes clear, he regards the first as the imperative basis for the second. For Harriman the assertion of the equality of rights, opportunities and liberties is not just a weapon to be employed self-righteously against the Communist dictatorships; it is an ideal to be fulfilled in the United States. Because he is at bottom an idealist himself—an idealist, as John Kennedy would say, without illusions—he has understood the necessity of idealism in America and the influence of ideals in the world. In the long run, in his view, ideals and not arms remain the greatest source of American power. But they can be effective only in so far as America tries to live up to her own highest standards.

He represents a bridge between the centuries, uniting perennial youthfulness of mind and demeanor with the characteristics of an older time—not only the distinction of manner but the brusque impatience with nonsense, the contempt for cant and the anger at complacency. His own memoirs of the bridge of years between Benjamin Harrison and Richard Nixon should be one of the most fascinating and instructive of American autobiographies. In the meantime, we can be grateful for the passages of reminiscence with which, in this book, he reinforces and illuminates a wise and modest interpretation of our times.

Arthur M. Schlesinger, Jr.

FOREWORD

This book is somewhat of an accident. It developed from an invitation last winter from Lehigh University to give the Blaustein lectures. These lectures had been established by Jacob Blaustein, a man whom I admire. He was ever ready to be helpful as an adviser to the State Department while I was at work there, and has supported generously many fine causes I believe in. This attracted me, and then, too, the arrangements for the lectures were appealing, especially the understanding that they would be published.

My difficulty in undertaking writing these days is that I am so much involved with the problems of the day. I am so frustrated by the continuation of the fighting in Vietnam that I feel I must do all I can to work for the end of this tragic war. Then, too, there are many national problems that concern me greatly these days. Throughout my life I have been active in things that I thought were important to our country—whether in business or in government. I have never been a good back seat rider and still have the urge to participate in the current battles.

When I learned from Professor Joynt, who was responsible for the lectures, that he was willing to agree to my subject, "United States-Soviet Union in a Changing World," to be given in three parts—past, present, future—I accepted.

The subject has been so much in my mind that I can talk about it without special preparation, and I delivered the lectures from brief notes. I have found that in speaking it is much more effective not to have a paper between you and the audience. If one finds the subject is appealing, one can amplify it. On the other hand, if one finds some idea is not getting across or is not having a good reception, one can cut it short and not have to drone on through the prepared sentences that fall like a wet blanket on the audience.

I want to express my appreciation for the hospitality of Dr. W. Deming Lewis, president of Lehigh, Dr. Carey Joynt, the trustees, the members of the Blaustein family, and the faculty and students for their cordial welcome.

I met with a number of student groups at private sessions beginning at breakfast—not my best hour—and filling every available moment until I was permitted a few hours of sleep. The students had a special interest in me because of my connection with the peace talks with the North Vietnamese in Paris. Then, too, I had excellent advance billing by Vice President Spiro Agnew in his attack on me, for which I am duly grateful. He has helped me bridge the generation gap.

Lehigh students, like most students I have spoken to, have a deep concern for Vietnam. Although Lehigh has not been subject to disruptive student explosion, the students are profoundly concerned about the war and want to see it ended. I firmly believe that the first disillusionment of students with the "Establishment" was their belief that our participation in the war in Vietnam was wrong, against our national interests, and without moral justification. With this disillusionment in the good judgment of their elders, the students began to question more and more critically other deficiencies in our national life. Their skepticisms were aroused by the thought that if anybody could be so wrong about the Vietnamese war, they must be wrong about most everything else. I am not suggesting that if the war is ended the students will relax and return to the normal lethargy that students have usually exhibited toward national affairs. The students of this generation are determined to see that things they think wrong are corrected, and they are going to have a hand in the doing of it.

I must hasten to add that, of course, I utterly reject extremists who destroy with no thought of building. I am speaking of the main sober body who, I believe, is now coming to the fore and will play a constructive role in the life of our country. Anyway, I hope so.

I was attracted to give these lectures because I find myself, as always, opposed to some so-called experts, who take extreme positions about the Soviet Union. On the one hand, I decry the old cold war warrior who sees no change, who still thinks in terms of the Stalin era with the monolithic structure of international Communism looming as the immediate threat it used to be. The dangers today are not at all the same. The monolithic structure of international Communism is shattered beyond repair and we can destroy ourselves if we do not understand the change. The other extreme I also decry are those who believe that now the only difference between us and the Soviets is a matter of economic theory and that all we have to do is show love and affection for them and everything will be all right.

I thought these lectures would give me an opportunity to express my views and explain why I reject both groups. And by publishing them, I was looking forward hopefully to attracting sufficient attention to be torn apart by the wrath of the standard-bearers of each extreme. I thought, too, that the question-and-answer periods would give me an opportunity to learn what the students were thinking about and to sharpen my mind to things that concerned them the most.

I thoroughly enjoyed my visit to Lehigh and got a great deal out of it—more I am sure than I left.

I was aghast, however, when I got the transcript of the lectures. My hope that it would be easy to edit it for publication was shattered. I found that in the three hour-long lectures and the answer periods I had touched on such a wide variety of subjects, that I had not been able to explain them fully in the time available. If recorded as given, they would lead to a good deal of misunderstanding and justifiable criticism. I had also left out some matters I thought pertinent. I have been assisted out of this dilemma by the editors of Doubleday, who suggested that rather than attempt to rewrite the lectures, I adopt the format used in this book. Under this format, I have not only been able to follow the structure of the lectures as given and keep the conversational style of an extemporaneous speech; but I have also been able to add explanations, amplifications, additional thoughts, and anecdotes. The original lecture appears in the same type as this foreword, and the additional materials appear in the sans-serif type, so they can be clearly identified.

I am not suggesting that these lectures, even with the additions, are in any sense a full analysis of the subject. Such an undertaking would take a number of volumes and endless research. Rather, I have tried to deal with the subject in broad brush strokes, using my own observations and deductions from my personal conversations and experiences. I have found that even this task has taken months of arduous struggle, particularly as I have attempted to express my thoughts with brevity.

When the Bolshevik Revolution occurred I felt that it would have a profound effect on world affairs during my lifetime and have therefore followed events in the Soviet Union quite closely over the years. I am not a Kremlinologist —a scholar who studies daily the outpourings of *Pravda* and other Soviet publications. I have great respect for their dedicated work and have learned much from them and their writings. I have been particularly influenced by my intimate personal experiences and talks over the years with leaders of the Soviet Union and other Communist countries. They have given me an insight into the continuing problems between the Soviet Union and the United States as they change with the shifting world and domestic scenes.

We are the only two countries that have the capacity to destroy each other and, incidentally, the better part of the world as well, in the doing. This gives both of us an incalculably heavy responsibility to find a way to get along on this small planet in spite of our differences.

I have tried to face up to this problem in these pages and to suggest ways we can realistically and effectively deal with it. The problem is confused by misunderstandings, rigid prejudices, and unrealistic hopes that exist in this country and by blind suspicions, misinformation, and inhuman ideology within the Soviet Union. The consequences of a conflict between us are so grave we cannot afford the luxury of being led astray by miscalculations or by indulging in emotions. Basically that is what this book is all about.

The lectures were given to engage the attention of thoughtful students, and this book is written for anyone who has a concern for our survival on this planet.

I owe a debt to many who have helped and worked with me over the years in Moscow, in other countries, and here at home. I particularly want to thank those who have read all or part of the manuscript and offered corrections and suggestions. First comes Mark Chadwin, who has worked diligently with me on every aspect of the book and has patiently and with good humor weathered the storms of my frustrations. I am thankful, too, for the advice given by Adrian Fisher, Dan Davidson, and Peter Duchin. Then, I appreciate enormously Arthur M. Schlesinger's willingness to associate himself with this undertaking through his Introduction and his most generous observations.

I am deeply grateful to Jacob Blaustein for establishing the lectures at Lehigh University and Professor Carey Joynt for having engaged me in this enterprise.

PAST

MY FIRST DIRECT CONTACT WITH THE
Soviet Union began in the middle twenties. I took part in a
manganese mining concession in the Caucasus undertaken
by a private group. I became involved in this venture largely
because I had followed the Russian Revolution closely and
had thought it would be one of the most important influences
in my life. I wanted to understand the Revolution, and being
a businessman I thought the way to understand it was to do
business with the regime. An interesting coincidence is that
I am speaking on United States-Soviet relations here in Grace
Hall, named for Eugene Grace (former president of the
Bethlehem Steel Company). He was a good friend of mine
and we were associates in that concession.

The mining operation covered a large manganese deposit
at Tchiaturi in the Caucasus mountains in Georgia.[1] Before
the Revolution this area had been shipping more manganese
ore than any other in the world. It had been operated by
a number of small owners. Our concession covered the
whole area and permitted the consolidation of the operations. We had built a modern concentration plant and were
conducting a far more efficient operation than in the past.
Although the government had expropriated the properties
from the previous owners, we felt they should be compen-
sated, and made an agreement to give them a certain percentage of our profits.

[1] Editor's Note: The passages in this type were not in the original lectures
but have been added by the author for this book.

The operations were going reasonably well but we were having certain difficulties with some of the terms of the concession. I went to Moscow to discuss these questions with government officials in December 1926. I had an opportunity to talk to Trotsky and other government leaders of that time. Stalin was Secretary of the Communist Party and didn't see many foreigners. Although I tried, I did not meet him. It was claimed that he was out of town. But I saw many others and got a strong impression of what was going on, and I became convinced of several things.

Under Lenin's New Economic Policy (the NEP), the Soviets were giving limited freedom to certain domestic private enterprises and to agriculture. In addition they were making contracts with foreign concessionaires to help develop their resources for a period of twenty years, after which the government planned to take over the operation. While in Moscow, I gained the impression that the NEP was on the way out. Stalin, as Secretary of the Party, was intriguing to take over the control of the government, and I gathered he opposed the NEP internally (particularly as it related to agriculture) as well as foreign concessions. He was determined that the Soviet government itself would control all operations in Russia.

Trotsky had been demoted from Commissar of Defense to Chairman of the Concessions Committee. I had a four-hour talk with him in this capacity about our concession and certain amendments we were proposing. We went over the concession agreement in detail, paragraph by paragraph. His mind was like a steel trap; he understood rapidly what I was talking about but in no way revealed his own attitude on what I had said.

The operations of the concession were going reasonably

well but we saw difficulties ahead because the Soviet Union was developing a new manganese mine at Nikopol, in the Ukraine north of Odessa. Since the production from our concession was a large percentage of world manganese consumption, it seemed evident that this new development would affect the world price of manganese unless we reduced our shipments to offset those from Nikopol. We were, therefore, proposing that the basis of the royalty be changed from a fixed sum per ton to a share of the profits. We recognized that the Soviet government wanted the maximum foreign exchange possible regardless of profit to pay for urgently needed imports. We therefore thought that our proposal, which would permit greater shipments at a lower price, served the Soviet government's interests as well as our own.

Trotsky listened attentively, asked some penetrating questions about prices and the world market, but gave me no indication of his own reaction. At the end of each point he asked me politely whether I had anything further to say, and when I replied in the negative he proceeded to the next one. After we had concluded the analysis of our concession he asked me if I had anything further to add. When I indicated I had concluded, he got up and shook hands with me.

During the four hours he had not made any personal remarks or brought up any extraneous subject. This seemed so extraordinary that I could not help believing that he was concerned over what might be recorded of his talk with me and its possible effect on his already doubtful position.

After shaking hands Trotsky turned on his heel and walked toward the door through which he had entered. I was taken to another door by our interpreter, George Andreichin, with whom I had a few minutes' conversation on the way out. Andreichin was an interesting character, having been educated with the Crown Prince of Bulgaria. He turned revolutionist and fled to the United States where he joined the IWW. During World War I he was arrested for refusing military service. He jumped his bail and went to Moscow. Later, during the purges of the thirties he was sent to a prison camp for having worked with Trotsky. After his release I saw him again in Moscow during the war. He then told me of Trotsky's concern about being tainted by what he might say to me.

During my talks in Moscow I visited Leningrad briefly. Prewar Leningrad was one of the most beautiful of Europe's cities. The silver spires on its churches were unique. It has been restored from wartime devastation with meticulous care and still retains much of its original charm.

When my talks in Moscow were concluded, I made a trip to the mines at Tchiaturi. I decided to behave like a capitalist and asked for a private car on the train, which was given to me. It was one of czarist vintage, most ornate and elaborately decorated. The fifteen-hundred-mile trip from Moscow to Baku took about four days. It was intensely interesting. The track was appallingly rough, but the twenty-five-mile-an-hour speed made it reasonably safe. I had a chance to see the countryside and the Russian people who crowded all the railroad stations. A particular tragedy of the time were the *bezprizornye*—the hundreds of thousands, perhaps millions of waif children orphaned by the Civil War. Many stayed in Moscow seeking almost any shelter in the bitter cold. There were more and more of them the farther south we went, begging or stealing and living as wild animals unconnected with the normal community life. Shortly afterward the Soviet government undertook to rehabilitate them. They were taken into boarding schools, orphanages, and, the more unruly, reformatories, where they were educated and taught trades. One hears that most of them became constructive members in the life of the country. Some, however, became part of the criminal world. At the time the tragic problem of these children seemed unsolvable.

We stopped off for a day or two at Tiflis, now Tiblisi, the capital of the Georgian republic. The American Relief, who were still working in the area, hospitably put us up as there were not hotel accommodations available at that time. The local officials took me to what they called the state wine library. It had been the wine cellar of Grand Duke Nicholas and, I believe, had been used for many years to help improve local wines by providing foreign wines for comparison. I was amazed by the quality of the cellar. We were given to taste a real Napoleon brandy, a Rhine wine of the 1860s still in splendid condition, an excellent French Bordeaux of 1906 and a number of their local vintages. By the time we emerged from the cellar we knew no pain. The government has continued to work on the improvement of their wines, and one can get in Moscow today a fine Caucasian red or white wine. They compare favorably even with some of the better European wines.

At the mines I met with our engineers and found they were well satisfied with the operations but had the usual problems with the government and railroad bureaucracies. As none of them spoke Russian, they had employed as interpreters and secretaries young educated Russian women of bourgeois background. They were glad to have the jobs, as it was hard for that class to get work. However, after our concession ended they were under suspicion for having worked for us and some were exiled. We tried to keep in touch with them and their families and assist them financially, but one of the tragedies of the operation was the unhappiness that came to these intelligent and decent people.

I tried to call on the mayor in Tchiaturi but he evidently

was terrified to see me and had vanished when I got to his office.

We returned on a Danish ore freighter through the Black Sea to Constantinople. It was a delightful relaxation after the strenuous trip to steam at ten knots for four days on the calm and beautiful water. After the backwardness of the Caucasian cities, Constantinople looked like the most modern and well kept of cities. It was a relief, too, to be out of the atmosphere of suspicion and fear.

As a result of my observations, I recommended to my colleagues on my return that we negotiate the withdrawal from the concession even though it was still making money. This we did after about a year of intensive negotiation and we got our investment out with a small profit. Other concessionaires who tried to hold on later lost heavily. Eugene Grace's profits from the concession were certainly not enough to build this hall, but perhaps they contributed a stone or two to it.

I learned a lot from the experience. I became convinced that the Bolshevik Revolution was in fact a reactionary revolution and that it was not "the wave of the future." It denied the basic beliefs that we value so deeply—the rights and dignity of the individual, the idea that government should express the will of the people. The Bolshevik conception was that the few knew what was good for the many and ruthlessly forced their will on the people. The individual was the servant of the state. Nothing has happened since to alter my conviction that the Bolshevik Revolution, for all its manifest achievements, has been on balance a tragic step backward in human development.

In dealing with developments in the Soviet Union and in the United States and our relations in a changing world, I am going to talk about the past, then the present, and finally take a shot at the future. Yet the past, the present, and the future are a running stream and can't be clearly divided. And I must warn you that in talking about the future I am not going to play the role of prophet. I learned another lesson in 1926. I asked a friend of mine, a Texan, who had just come back from Moscow what was going to happen in the Soviet Union. He replied, "I feel about Russia the way we do about the weather in Texas. Anyone who tries to predict the weather in Texas is a newcomer."

At that time people generally were still predicting that the Revolution in Russia would not survive for more than five years. Each year the forecast continued to be five years. On this visit I became convinced that for better or worse the Soviet regime was here to stay.

Before going to Moscow I had talked to many people at home, in European governments and in our embassies. However, of all those I talked to I found the best informed and the clearest analysts were the American and British correspondents then in Moscow. Among these were Walter Duranty of the New York *Times* and H. R. Knickerbocker of the New York *Evening Post*, and since then Henry Shapiro of UPI. Incidentally, I learned in my other travels, both as a businessman and a government representative that our foreign correspondents were a most important source of information. I have, therefore, always made it a point to see them, and although they came to interview me, in the process I interviewed them. In recent years I have found this particularly true in Saigon.

There have been of course marked changes within the Soviet Union since that time. It is important that we recognize and try to understand the significance of these developments.

In those early days—the mid-twenties—I found in Moscow a freer atmosphere than later. During the revolutionary terror many of the bourgeoisie had been killed or had fled the country, but those that remained were living more normally though still under the watchful eye of the GPU (the secret police). In the arts there was a revolutionary spirit, even though before his death Lenin had begun to criticize modern abstractionism as being only for the intellectual elite and not for the proletariat. There was still free expression, but in writing at least a bow had to be given to Communist ideology. Foreign books and publications were not prohibited. Excitement existed about the new theater and in other fields. Isadora Duncan's expressive dancing was in vogue. Later Stalin killed all that. He replaced any revolutionary spirit in artistic expression with what is called "socialist realism." With few exceptions, art became a sterile form of promoting ideological propaganda and socialist purpose.

The government commissars I called on showed real interest in talking with me since not many American businessmen had come to Moscow. They discussed their problems. They explained the difficulty of applying Marxian concepts to agricultural Russia. The Marxist Revolution was intended to be undertaken in an industrial society rather than an agricultural one. The ambition of a peasant was, after all, to become a landowner—a capitalist. It was the oppressed industrial worker that could be inspired to embrace the class struggle. If only they were able to take over Germany—or even the United States, they said, they could more readily achieve their Communist objectives. In addition there was concern at the time because of the Marxist-Leninist conception that a single Communist state could not exist for long in a capitalist world.

Stalin rejected both concerns. He clashed with Trotsky on ideological differences. Trotsky thought in terms of dogmatic Communist theory and world revolution, whereas Stalin recognized the prospect for international revolution were then dim and was determined to transform and dominate Russia. Through his close contact with party members and his development of the party apparatus Stalin intrigued to force Trotsky out. He ruthlessly undertook the immense and cruel tasks of communizing the peasant through collectivizing the farms. There was going to be Communism in the Soviet Union, and Moscow was going to be the center of Communism in the world.

The commissars I saw were all very keen to get United States recognition, and I felt that when President Roosevelt did recognize them in 1933 we did not drive as hard a bargain as we might have on some issues.

I had pointed out to the Soviet commissars in 1926 that the difficulty in American public opinion regarding recognition was, first and foremost, the support and money coming from Moscow for Communist subversive activities in the United States. They insisted that the Soviet government had nothing to do with this, that the Communist Party was entirely independent of the Soviet government. I would have none of it. I asserted that the Communist Party and the Soviet government were one and the same.

Another difficulty we discussed was the financial claims and counterclaims of the United States Government and its nationals and the Soviet government. They claimed heavy damage for the alleged effects of American intervention in 1918. I maintained that all of these had to be negotiated out in a sensible manner. These claims and counterclaims were dealt with in the 1933 exchange of letters establishing relations with the Soviet Union.

Also, in these letters Soviet government intervention in United States internal affairs was prohibited. The prohibition of government action was described in considerable detail, but action by the Russian Communist Party or the Comintern was not specifically mentioned. I felt at the time that this should have been done, but looking back at it I doubt that such a provision would have made much difference. This is the kind of thing that is too easily evaded to be fully enforceable.

Then the war came. I am not going to go into the events which led to the war. Chamberlain hoped to direct Hitler to the East and was unsuccessful. Stalin hoped to reverse the direction of Hitler's attack by his infamous agreement with Hitler dividing Poland. But he succeeded only temporarily. On June 22, 1941, Hitler turned on him.

Stalin talked about these events on more than one occasion during the many times I saw him during the war.

At times he was explicit, at others he was evasive. He criticized Chamberlain for not having consulted him on a high enough level to be convincing. He contended that prior to Munich he would have been willing to join in resisting Hitler's aggression against Czechoslovakia. He gave these as excuses for his deal with Hitler. He evidently thought that the British and American intelligence information of Hitler's plans for attack on Russia given him as early as April 1941 was an attempt to trick him into actions that would provoke war between Russia and Germany. He intimated that he had not mobilized in the face of German deployments on the Russian border, believing that it would have given Hitler a pretext for breaking their agreement. He claimed that he had been doing everything he could to improve the Red Army's ability to resist a possible attack but was not yet ready in 1941. He said once, "If Hitler had only given me one more year."

It seems that Stalin could not bring himself to believe that Hitler would attack when he did. He evidently became rattled, then blamed Molotov and others for the disaster. It has been reported that it was some days before he grasped control of the situation again.

When Hitler attacked Russia on June 22, Churchill announced immediately, in a radio broadcast to the British, acceptance of the Soviet Union as an ally. He declared, "Any man or state who fights on against Nazidom will have our aid. . . ." In a comment to an associate, he said, "If Hitler invaded Hell I would make at least a favorable reference to the Devil in the House of Commons."

To me news of Hitler's diversion to the East came as a most welcome relief even though we were not yet in the war. I was in Cairo at the time and was seeing firsthand how hard pressed the British were on the Western Desert as a result of Rommel's offensives. Crete had just fallen after the British gallant but hopeless attempt to help the Greeks. I had been with Churchill at the time of the British decision to fulfill their treaty commitment to support Greece, and I recall his saying, "Britain can afford to lose a battle but not her honor."

Although the British did not succeed in saving Greece, they did rally the Greek defense, slowing up the German advance. This, together with the courageous Yugoslav resistance, set back Hitler's timetable for the attack on Russia by more than five weeks. This delay probably saved Moscow from being taken before winter set in. The Germans were not well prepared for winter warfare. The loss of Moscow might well have knocked Russia out of the war as an effective fighting force.

I was then in the Middle East at the request of Churchill, and with the President's approval, to report on how we could help strengthen the British forces in the area through Lend-Lease supplies and other actions. President Roosevelt had sent me to London four months before to advise him on what we could do short of war to help the British hold out. We were assisting the British not only with supplies under Lend-Lease but in other ways, including naval escort of their convoys over halfway across the North Atlantic.

After my return from the Middle East, our Air Force took over from the RAF the cross-Africa air ferry route from West Africa to Khartoum and then down the Nile to Egypt. Our Navy cleared the port of Massawa of sunken Italian vessels and made this important naval base on the Red Sea operational again. We sent such military materiel as we could spare—particularly heavy trucks and some tanks.

For a year since the fall of France, the British had been standing alone against the full force of the Nazi power under air attack and threat of invasion. It was a great relief for them that Hitler had turned to the East and Russia was now an ally.

President Roosevelt believed that it was in our interest to support Churchill's position toward Russia, and he sent Harry Hopkins to London to take stock of the war situation in light of recent developments. In spite of the pessimistic forecast of the military that the Russians could not hold out for more than a few months, Churchill and Hopkins thought that it would be useful for Hopkins to go to Moscow and talk to Stalin. Roosevelt agreed that Hopkins should go and report back to both men. It was a dramatic moment when Hopkins left Churchill Sunday evening July 27 at Chequers for his

WINGATE COLLEGE LIBRARY
WINGATE N. C.

train trip to Scotland and then the long, dangerous flight to Archangel—a twenty-seven-hour non-stop flight in one of the slow PBY "flying boats." Hopkins' journey to Moscow seemed to us at that time about as remote and hazardous as a trip to the moon today.

I saw Hopkins again at the Atlantic Conference on August 7, the meeting of Roosevelt and Churchill "at sea." I had come up from Washington, and Hopkins had arrived with Churchill on the H.M.S. *Prince of Wales*. Hopkins brought with him a list of urgent requirements Stalin had given him. But more importantly from his observations and his long talks with Stalin he reported his belief, at variance with the general military appraisal, that the Russians would hold out. As a result Roosevelt and Churchill decided to send American and British missions to negotiate with Stalin a program of supply. Lord Beaverbrook, Minister of Supply and a member of the British War Cabinet, and I were selected to head them.

Henry Morgenthau, Secretary of Treasury, and Frank Knox, Secretary of the Navy, each thought the President was going to appoint him to head the American Mission. Both discussed the subject with me, but the President decided to send me. I think it was because he knew that I could work with Beaverbrook—not always easy—and then, too, that I clearly understood his own objectives.

Roosevelt and Churchill had a deep interest to keep Russia in the war. To this end assistance to Russia was essential.

For over a year Churchill and Britain had been bearing the full brunt of the force of the Nazi power. They needed the Soviet Union as an ally. For their own self-preservation, they wanted to keep the Russians fighting. The two and one half years I spent in Britain was one of the most extraordinarily rewarding periods that I have ever had. Every man, woman, and child in Britain had one objective, and that was to hold out under the inspired leadership of Churchill. There was no other thought. There was no other objective. I doubt if ever in history there has been a nation as united as that nation was at that time.

In addition to helping Britain, Roosevelt had another consideration in mind. We were not in the war at the time, yet he feared that sooner or later we would be, although he didn't know how. He was anxious, however, that if we did get involved, our participation would be limited to air and naval power with a minimum of ground forces. We are all, to a considerable extent, the product of our experience, and Roosevelt had a horror of the trench warfare of World War I. He didn't want to see American men sent to the Continent to go through that type of warfare again. He hoped that if we could help the Russians continue to fight, the Red Army would be able to keep the Axis armies engaged, and by using our air and sea power we could avoid committing major ground forces on the continent of Europe. That did not prove possible, but I think it was a factor in his decision to give direct support to Russia at that time. Of course the Red Army did prove to be a vital force in the defeat of Hitler.

So the prime objective of Beaverbrook's and my missions in September 1941 was to find out what the Russians needed and to come to some understanding with Stalin on what we might be able to supply. Some of my colleagues on the staff flew to Moscow in two converted B-24 bombers, a tough thirty-two-hundred-mile flight, the longest distance the U. S. Army had flown passengers. Together with the members of both our missions, I went with Beaverbrook by sea on the British cruiser H.M.S. *Lincoln*. We sailed unescorted, relying on the speed of the ship and an extreme northern route (north of Bear Island) to avoid German submarines and aircraft attack. We received messages from London and Moscow but could not reply for fear of giving away our location.

This fact led to a tempest in a teapot over my taking Quentin Reynolds with me to handle press relations. Stafford Cripps, the British Ambassador in Moscow, sent a message to Churchill, which I could read but not answer, that the whole mission would be undermined if Reynolds were allowed to come on my staff. He contended that the Soviet government had refused Reynolds a visa and that his hitchhiking to Moscow with me would create disastrous suspicion. Of course, I had gotten a visa for Quent just before we left London, which Cripps hadn't known. His interventions led to messages back and forth to Moscow, creating a lot of trouble for nothing. I was, of course, indignant at Cripps's action and told him so when we got to Moscow. Beaverbrook was delighted. He always loved squabbles and especially about Cripps, with whom he personally had little rapport (to indulge in a British understatement).

I had asked Quent to join my mission particularly because he was a Catholic. The President wanted me to impress on Stalin how important it was to ease restrictions on religion. Roosevelt was concerned about possible opposition from religious groups to congressional action to include the Soviet Union under Lend-Lease. In addition, he sincerely wanted to use our wartime collaboration to modify Soviet antagonism toward religion. In fact he stated to the press in Washington while I was in Moscow that he had instructed me to raise this subject.

Although Stalin and every Soviet official nodded when I broached the subject, the most action I could get was a statement by Commissar of Information Lozovski. He noted the President's reference to the guarantee of religious freedom in the Soviet Union constitution and asserted that religious freedom was fully permitted. Roosevelt did not think that was enough, and I felt he was critical of my failure to get more. In fact although for reasons of domestic morale during the war there was some relaxation of discrimination against the religious faithful, there has been no fundamental change in Communist ideological opposition to religion.

Quentin Reynolds, however, proved to be of great help in keeping our Moscow correspondents reasonably happy as I had little time to spend with them. In addition he stayed on as a journalist for some weeks and was permitted to travel rather extensively. He reported vividly about the courage and determination of the Russian people under the desperate hardships of the Nazi invasion.

On arrival in Archangel we flew on to Moscow in two Soviet transport planes, copies of the American DC-3, with a fighter escort. It was a rough trip as the Russian pilots flew under the low hanging clouds. They had no navigational aids and navigated by the lay of the land. It was literally treetop flying. And when we were shot at by a Soviet anti-aircraft battery, which had not been informed of our flight, we seemed to fly *between* the trees.

In Moscow we found that Stalin was ready to see us that same evening. I acceded to Beaverbrook's suggestion that we ask for Litvinov as the sole interpreter. Beaverbrook thought it might encourage Stalin to greater frankness if he and I went alone. Both of us had confidence that Litvinov would do an accurate job. I had met him in 1926 when he was Deputy Foreign Minister. In the intervening years he had been Foreign Minister and then had fallen from favor.

During the week we were in Moscow, the German forces were threatening the city. You could hear the guns at the front and the American military attache thought that Moscow was doomed and that we had better get out quickly. While we were in Moscow Hitler announced the opening of the final drive on Moscow, and his press spokesman stated a few days later, "For all military purposes Soviet Russia is done with." It did look pretty desperate. But Stalin was utterly determined. With all his ruthlessness he led the defense of Moscow, then the reconstruction of the armies, and the eventual victory.

After a drive through the deserted streets of Moscow in the "blackout," it was an eerie moment when we approached the awesome Kremlin gates, and our car was stopped. The guards took a good look at us, shining flashlights in our faces to make sure who we were. Then we were allowed to proceed to the building in which Stalin had his office.

This was the first of many talks I had with Stalin during the next four years. I was struck by how short he was. He was a man of few words, almost detached, except when he became interested; then he showed strong attitudes, sometimes emotion, at times brutally blunt, at others emphatically frank. At times he appeared to evade your eye, at others, particularly when he wanted to see your reaction, he looked straight at you with a cold and penetrating stare. Sometimes he drew pictures on a pad, doodling. At one time during the talks with Beaverbrook and myself when he appeared annoyed, he drew pictures of wolves and then filled in the background with red pencil.

We had three long talks on successive evenings. During the first meeting he discussed the military situation and his urgent requirements, and Beaverbrook and I outlined what was available from British and American sources. Stalin appeared so agreeable that Beaverbrook was elated and thought our job was almost done. In the second talk, however, after Stalin had a chance to review what we had said with his colleagues, he was brutally critical, claiming gruffly that the paucity of our offers was proof that we wanted the Soviet Union defeated.

It was hard sledding. He argued about individual items, about which he was particularly concerned. He refused to accept our explanations. For example, at one time he turned on me, saying, "Why is it that the United States can only offer one thousand tons of armor plate for tanks, a country with a production of over fifty million tons of steel?" He brushed aside my explanation of the length of time required to increase capacity for this type of steel, saying, "One only has to add some alloys."

Beaverbrook and I left the meeting puzzled and somewhat discouraged. We decided to give Stalin during the third talk, as a response to the list of Soviet requirements they had given us, an itemized statement of categories of equipment and material we believed we could furnish. Stalin evidently felt that he had put as much pressure on us as he could and now accepted our offer with good grace. He even showed enthusiasm. He emphasized the urgent need for trucks, particularly three-ton trucks were "the most desirable." "Our bridges can't carry any heavier," he said. He also expressed concern about barbed wire. I assured him we would give his requests full consideration and do all we could.

I talked to Stalin about our use of Siberian airfields if we got into trouble with Japan. He indicated this would be given consideration and agreed to give us information about their location and facilities. In talking about Japan Stalin commented, "Japan is not like Italy, willing to be a serf of Germany, and can be won away." He criticized the Chinese Nationalist government "for not fighting" but said that he was continuing to send some help as his neutrality treaty with Japan did not specifically exclude it.

During these difficult talks with Stalin, Beaverbrook had shown great skill and sensitivity. He was a faithful colleague throughout, and I gained an increased respect and affection for him.

Molotov was assigned the task of drafting with us a protocol covering our understanding. In our earlier meetings with Molotov he had established six working committees. Our colleagues together with Soviet officials had analyzed in detail the Soviet requests—munitions, raw materials, and food. I made it clear to Stalin that the materials listed in the protocol were not a definite commitment but were what we would make every effort to supply. There was no agreement on terms of repayment since the Congress had not as yet extended Lend-Lease to include the Soviet Union.

I got an interesting sidelight on the Kremlin reaction from a talk I had with Mikoyan on the details of their raw material requirements. He said, "We have complete confidence in your good intentions because you have been so careful in your promises."

Stalin put his seal of approval on our discussions by inviting us to a banquet in the Kremlin just before we left. In my notes at the time I described the dinner:

Our dinner turned out to be for over a hundred people including all of our Mission and our B-24 aviators, the British Mission, and some of the embassy staffs with the Russian delegates and other Russian officials.

I arrived ten minutes late and Beaverbrook twenty. Stalin came in almost immediately after Beaverbrook's arrival with Voroshilov[2] and Mikoyan. He walked down the long room used as the dining room into the smaller room where we were gathered. His greeting was formal, and he shook hands with

[2] Marshal Kliment Voroshilov, member of the State Defense Committee, former Commissar of Defense and long-time intimate of Stalin.

everyone with whom he came in contact although there was no line formed for introductions.

Dinner began shortly. There was a head table stretched the length of the room at which Stalin sat, Beaverbrook on his right and I on his left, Molotov on my left and Litvinov on Beaverbrook's right and the members of our Missions and the Russian commissars and the two ambassadors stretched along the balance of the table—making a total of about thirty with no one sitting opposite.

On the other side of the red carpet down the middle of the room there were four tables seating about eighteen at right angles to the head table.

The room was called the Catherine the Great Room and had an "E" ["Ekaterina"] on the shields at the head of the columns. It was highly decorated—gilt carving and small painted shields at intervals around the room of some subject which I thought was religious, but they were so high I could not tell. The walls were white plaster and the floor a good hardwood. The curtains across the windows were, I believe, red and in perfect condition—in fact the entire room was in a state of perfect repair. The only carpet was the red runner down the center connecting at one end with the old ballroom, which had been rebuilt into an enormous meeting room for the Supreme Soviet, and the other end with the anteroom in which we had met.

The dinner was the usual affair of endless hors d'oeuvres beginning with caviar and various forms of fish, cold suckling pig, then the main courses of hot soup, chicken and a game bird, with ice cream and cakes for dessert. There were various types of fruit not available on the public market.

In front of each man were a number of bottles containing pepper vodka, red and white wine, a Russian brandy—and champagne brought in at the time of the sweet.

Stalin drank his first toast in pepper vodka, only part of the glass, then poured the balance of it out into one of his larger glasses and for the rest of the meal drank wine in this glass, filling it himself frequently. The glass was very small, about the size of a double pony of brandy. When the champagne came he drank this out of the same glass. He put one of his other glasses over the champagne bottle in order, he said, to keep in the bubbles. . . .

He was relaxed and kept looking around the room. He talked to Beaverbrook and seemed to be enjoying himself. . . .

Beaverbrook talked to him about English people—Lady Astor and George Bernard Shaw and such Americans as George Howard. The conversation was superficial but rather genial. . . .

Rather late in the dinner Stalin said that the war should be won by the armies of the three countries meeting. I said that I agreed and he turned and shook my hand.

On my asking about the war news he said there were difficulties in the south. The Crimea was strong now as it was reinforced by troops that had been taken from Odessa. Leningrad news was better. . . .

When a toast was made to the two American pilots who had flown the B-24s to Moscow, Stalin went all the way around the table to the center of the room to meet the two men, with his glass in his hand. . . . That was Stalin's way of showing special favor.

The toasts were over thirty in number. . . . During the toasts Stalin would stand up with his glass on the table and when he liked the sentiment of the toast, which was in most cases, he clapped his hands and then drank his toasts. . . .

We subsequently were shown two movies in a beautiful little theater in the same building. . . .

. . . The first movie was a war picture made, they said, two years before. The second was a comedy about a theatrical troupe on a trip on the Volga which included some rather good singing. Stalin appeared to enjoy particularly the music.

Stalin made it very plain that the Russians would go on fighting. He believed they could hold Moscow. He said Hitler had made a mistake in not driving with full force directly to the capital. Instead he had attacked on a three-prong drive—one to Leningrad, one to Moscow, and one southeast toward the oil fields.

If Hitler had concentrated on Moscow, Stalin said, he could have taken the city, and if Moscow had fallen the nerve center of the nation would have been destroyed. The Russians would go on fighting, Stalin added, but they would have to retreat to the Urals and would be impotent to undertake any offensive action. He was very frank about the difficulties but very determined to hold out.

So we did begin to send them supplies. Much of the military matériel that we sent them at first was diverted from the British because our production at that time—late 1941—was extremely limited. Later on the flow became considerably greater. The food, which we sent promptly, was of great importance, even to those who were in Leningrad during the appalling siege. Some of the food got there and helped them hold out. As time went on our supplies became an increasingly important factor. Stalin at Teheran emphasized his great respect for American industry, saying, "Without the United States as a source of motors, this war would have been lost."

Beginning in late 1941 Stalin was consistently demanding a second front, first from Britain and after Pearl Harbor from us both. He was aware of Churchill's greater caution than ours about a cross-Channel operation. Fearing a serious misunderstanding with Stalin, Churchill decided in July 1942 that he should go to Moscow himself to explain the military situation to Stalin, why the invasion of France could not be undertaken that year, and to inform him of the plans for TORCH, the North African operation. At Churchill's suggestion Roosevelt approved my going along but sent me no other instructions.

I joined Churchill in Cairo where he was reviewing the military situation. It was gratifying to see some of our equipment, which we had sent as a result of my visit a year earlier, arriving and in use.

We went on to Teheran and from there to Moscow. I flew with Churchill in his B-24 with his American pilot. It was converted for passengers in the most primitive manner, without insulation, and with two rows of hard benches facing each other. The noise was so great it made conversation impossible. Our only communication was by passing notes to each other, some on important subjects, some trivial.

Churchill, as always, was accompanied by his naval aide, Commander Thompson, who had a delightful personality but failed at times to make all arrangements in a manner satisfactory to the Prime Minister. When "Tommy" produced the lunch basket a major crisis arose. The Prime Minister selected a ham sandwich and then demanded mustard. The basket was turned upside down, but no mustard. Churchill wrote a note, "How could you have forgotten the mustard? No gentleman eats ham sandwiches without mustard." Tommy got back into the Prime Minister's good graces, however, on the return trip. This time the lunch basket was provided by the Kremlin and included caviar, champagne, and other delicacies. Churchill was delighted and wrote Tommy, "All is forgiven—even the mustard."

We could not take the direct route over Baku and Stalingrad because of the closeness of the Luftwaffe on the southern fronts.

Instead we flew well to the east over the Caspian to Kuibyshev and then on to Moscow.

After a formal reception by Molotov at the airport with a guard of honor, band, and arrival speeches, the Prime Minister was driven to a *dacha* put at his disposal. It was a comfortable country house in pine woods, half an hour out of Moscow. During his stay the "P.M." enjoyed the beautiful country setting with Moscow's sunny summer weather. A fish pond on the estate particularly amused him. He could feed the fish, a pastime he enjoyed at his own country home at Chartwell. I was given a largish guesthouse in Moscow. It was big enough for me to put up General Russel L. Maxwell, U. S. Commander in the Middle East, and General Sidney Spalding of Lend-Lease, both of whom at my request had come with me from Cairo. We were treated sumptuously with food and drink. It was particularly impressive to have caviar served at breakfast. Shortly after our arrival, I took our Ambassador, Admiral William H. Standley, out to call on the Prime Minister and learned Stalin had arranged to see us that evening. Admiral Standley was a little unhappy that he wasn't asked to come along but that was entirely impossible. I was there representing the President in a very personal capacity because of my direct relations with the Prime Minister in London.

Stalin received us in his Kremlin office. He wore a tunic-style jacket, pinkish pepper-colored, with greenish trousers pushed into well-worn boots. He looked a bit grayer and older than the previous year but still vigorous.

The room was long and not very wide with a desk at the far end. A globe was placed on one corner of it. A long narrow table ran along one wall of the room with windows on the opposite side. There were three enormous super-life-size photographs on the walls—one of course of Lenin and the other two of the bushy-bearded prophets of the faith—Marx and Engels. Rolls of maps hung on the wall behind the table.

The table itself could seat perhaps a couple of dozen people. Stalin invited us to sit down at one end of this table. I found myself next to Stalin with Churchill and his party opposite. A generous supply of cigarettes and bottled mineral water were on the table between us.

Churchill began the talk by asking for news of the front. Stalin said the situation around Moscow was "sound," but described the southern fronts in very somber tones. In the drive on Baku and on Stalingrad the Nazis had attacked in greater force than expected and had broken through the Red Army lines. Stalin said he did not know how Hitler had been able "to gather together so many troops and tanks." He felt sure that "Hitler had drained the whole of Europe." Stalin hoped to hold Stalingrad but could not be sure. The Red Army was undertaking a counterattack north of Moscow to try to divert some Nazi forces from the south fronts.

In this atmosphere Churchill had to undertake to explain that the second front in Europe, the cross-Channel operation, was not possible in 1942. He described why the required build-up of forces in the United Kingdom and from the United States with the necessary landingcraft could not be accomplished until the following year. Stalin argued with him at every turn, disputing Churchill's figures on German forces in the west and claiming that their divisions were under-strength—"only two regiments apiece." He said that his views about war were different: "Any man who is not prepared to take risks cannot win a war."

Churchill agreed but asserted it would be folly to waste troops which would be needed for a successful operation next year. Stalin finally appeared to accept the inevitable and stated with dignity that although he disagreed with Churchill's arguments against a landing in France, "I am not entitled to insist upon it."

Churchill then unfolded the TORCH operation, the invasion of North Africa in late October. He emphasized the possibilities that this opened up of knocking Italy out of the war. Drawing a picture of Europe in the shape of a crocodile with its hard snout in Brittany, he said we could attack "the soft underbelly." He emphasized the role the United States would play in the North African landings and, much to my surprise, asked me to explain them.

I supported what the Prime Minister had said and indicated that the President was pressing for as early a date as possible for the North African landings. I pointed out that in spite of the serious problems the President had in the Pacific, his first concern was the European war. Stalin showed increasing interest and asked a number of questions, particularly about possible political reaction in France and Spain.

While driving back to his dacha Churchill expressed himself as being highly pleased with the outcome of the meeting and thanked me for helping him over some of the rough spots. He said it was "the most important conference he had ever attended." At lunch the next day he suggested that he go to the next meeting with Stalin without me. He planned to take his three senior military officers with him. However, Stalin sent word that he wanted me to be present.

At this second meeting, beginning at eleven-fifteen at night, Stalin handed us a tough aide-memoire asserting that when Molotov had been in London in June a second front had been agreed to and that without it the situation of the Red Army was being prejudiced. It asserted again that a second front could and should be opened this year and that next year it could be more difficult. It was a shock to receive this memorandum considering what had been said the day before. Churchill made a strong statement denying any promise and said he would reply in writing to the aide-memoire. He explained again that the plans outlined would be the best way to assist Russia and that there would be no value in an undertaking "that would only lead to disaster." He then again turned to me.

I supported the Prime Minister and stated that these decisions had been reached after the most careful consideration. I said, "President Roosevelt believed they were in the interests of the Soviet cause" and was prepared to take action that offered "a reasonable prospect of success."

Stalin continued to argue that we were neglecting the support needed for the Russian front, at one point saying to Churchill, "The British Army should not be so frightened of the Germans." Churchill replied that he "only pardoned that remark on account of the bravery of the Russian Army." He told Stalin that he seemed "to overlook the existence of the Channel."

The Prime Minister gave a brilliant account of the year the British stood alone. In spite of Stalin's provocations, Churchill refrained from any reference to what Stalin was doing during that period. He continued emphatically at great length, forgetting about the need for interpretation. Finally, he permitted his interpreter to begin to translate what he had said, a difficult task at best, to find Russian phrases for Churchillian English. The interpreter was floundering and having such difficulty that Stalin interrupted: "Your words are of no importance. What is important is your spirit."

That incident broke the ice, and we began talking about other matters. Stalin had been disturbed by the decision to suspend the northern convoys to Murmansk and Archangel. The last convoy had had disastrous losses—twenty-three out of thirty-four ships had been sunk. I urged the expansion of the southern—Persian Gulf—route and suggested expanding aircraft deliveries through Alaska and Siberia. Churchill also raised the question of sending a British air force to support the Red Army in the Caucasus after the TORCH operation, about which Stalin showed real interest. Before we left, Stalin invited us to the Kremlin for dinner the following evening.

In my talks with the "P.M." that night and again the next day, he was deeply depressed. I tried to assure him that Stalin's tactics were similar to those he had used on Beaverbrook and myself the year before—being unreasonably rough and rude in our second meeting and then showing approval and even enthusiasm in the third. I told him I was sure Stalin would not want him to leave in an unfriendly mood.

The Kremlin banquet was less gay than the year before. Stalin included all the members of the Soviet Defense Committee as well as members of the General Staff. He, himself, was in the best of spirits and most cordial to the Prime Minister and myself. He seemed entirely oblivious of the unpleasant discussion of the night before. The Prime Minister, however, arrived still somewhat annoyed by the rough treatment he had received. Yet as the evening progressed he became more and more interested in his talk with Stalin, which ranged from the theory of military tactics to postwar policies.

On the lighter side, they talked about Nancy Astor's visit to Moscow in the thirties, during which she had told Stalin that Churchill was "done," whereas Stalin had maintained that, "If war comes, Churchill will be Prime Minister." Churchill commented that he had not been very friendly to the Soviet Union after the last war. Stalin replied, "I know, but you are always honest in your opposition." Churchill asked whether he was ready to forgive and forget all that. Stalin replied, "It is not a matter for me to forgive, it is for God to forgive."

I talked with Stalin about plans for a meeting between President Roosevelt and himself and discussed when and where it might take place. Stalin said, "It is of great importance," and suggested, "In the winter I am not so preoccupied." The possible places ranged from one of the Aleutian Islands to Iceland. (A meeting, in fact, eventually took place with all three —Roosevelt, Churchill, and Stalin—at Teheran in November 1943.)

Stalin made some unfavorable comments to me about the British Army but expressed admiration for the RAF. He showed bitterness against the British Navy for the suspension of the northern convoys. He had no understanding of the extreme difficulties in getting ships through.

Stalin for a time concentrated on personally toasting his generals with a favorable comment appropriate to each. The only foreigner to whom he offered a toast was President Roosevelt; all others were given by Molotov.

The next day, August 15, Churchill called on Stalin alone for a short talk and to say good-by. It turned out to be an all-night session. Stalin invited him to stay for dinner, and their talk continued for over seven hours. In fact there was only an hour or two between the end of this meeting and our departure for Teheran at 5:00 A.M. Churchill was highly gratified by the intimacy of this talk, and it established the personal relationship between the two men during the war.

Despite my many experiences with Churchill during the war, I gained in these days in Moscow an even higher respect and admiration for him, if that were possible. All his qualities of eloquence, determination, and yet restraint under provocation shone in the manner in which he faced and dealt with the crude Soviet dictator. It was a masterful performance throughout. He was the bearer of bad news to Stalin and yet left having gained his confidence. This laid the basis for successful wartime military collaboration so vital to the defeat of Hitler.

It is significant that Stalin kept his military commitments during the war. He had agreed that after we landed at Normandy in June 1944 he would attack in the east. People forget there were at the time about two hundred Nazi divisions and about fifty satellite divisions on the Eastern Front. Our plans were based on the premise that we could not land successfully in Normandy if there were more than about thirty mobile German divisions in the west of Europe. Therefore the transfer of a relatively small number of divisions from the Eastern Front to the west could have been disastrous.

One of the reasons why General Marshall and General Eisenhower believed for some time after the war that we could get along with the Russians, and why they were so reluctant to finally agree that we couldn't, was because Stalin had carried out his military commitments. The Red Army attacked in force, you remember, shortly after we landed and broke through the German lines.

It was not until the foreign Ministers' conference in Moscow in March 1947 that General Marshall, then Secretary of State, finally concluded that the cooperation we had envisioned with the Soviets was impossible. Even then, he included the Soviet Union and Eastern Europe in his offer of the Marshall Plan for European recovery.

From the political standpoint, Roosevelt and Churchill had in mind that we should use the wartime intimacies to develop a relationship with Stalin for the postwar world. Roosevelt believed that this Communist dictatorship was unnatural and that the rigid control could not last. He was a religious man himself, and he didn't believe the Russian people would be satisfied by an atheistic philosophy. He didn't believe that the

Kremlin could permanently control the minds of the people, nor that the Russian people would accept indefinitely that kind of complete control. So he felt that if we could get through a period of years working cooperatively, we would find in time that we would come closer together, and the differences, which were then great would be reduced. I agreed in principle, but I wasn't as optimistic about how long it would take.

I still believe that to be true, but it's a question of whether it's decades or generations. I became somewhat more hopeful when in January of 1968 I saw the Czech Communist Party itself adopt an entirely new liberal policy toward freedom of expression, and it is a great tragedy that it collapsed under the force of the Red Army.

During the war Roosevelt had two basic approaches. One was the over-all approach to work together for a peaceful postwar world. Roosevelt, having seen Wilson fail with his League of Nations, decided that we should develop a United Nations during the wartime and have the nations committed to it then, so that it would last in the postwar period. In this he was successful. The United Nations was established and, with all its limitations, it is still a force for peace and international collaboration.

Secondly, both he and Churchill (Churchill first) became concerned, realizing that the Red Army would occupy Eastern Europe. Nothing could stop that. The Red Army would drive the Nazi forces back into Germany and in the process would occupy these countries. Therefore, we had to make every effort to see that the peoples of those countries, after they were liberated, were allowed to establish their own governments and that they would not be forceably communized and made satellites of the Soviet Union.

Poland became one of the principal subjects of discussion.

It was important to the British because, as you remember, the British went to war when Hitler attacked Poland. It was important to Stalin because Poland was the invasion route from Europe into Russia, and Stalin insisted on having a friendly neighbor. He had in mind not only Hitler and Kaiser Wilhelm but Napoleon as well.

On Roosevelt's instructions I discussed the future of Poland with Stalin more often than any other single subject. Once, in March 1944, when I raised the subject Stalin said impatiently, "Again the Poles? Is that the most important question?" He added that he had been so occupied with the Poles that he had had "no time for military matters." I replied that the Polish question "was pressing." I pointed out that the American public opinion would not support a "hand-picked" government for Poland and that the Polish people should be "given a chance freely to choose their own government." Stalin replied that he was "concerned about public opinion in the Soviet Union." As our talks had been exceedingly direct, I commented, "You know how to handle your public opinion." He answered, "There have been three revolutions in a generation." Molotov, who rarely interjected himself into the conversation, added, "In Russia, there is an active public opinion which overthrows governments."

In speaking of three revolutions, Stalin, of course, was referring to the uprising in 1905, the Kerensky revolution of February 1917 and then the Bolshevik October Revolution the following autumn.

During that period there was a misunderstanding of the meaning of words between the Soviet Union and ourselves. You may blame all of us for not fully recognizing this. But it is easy to look back now and appreciate that to us "a friendly neighbor" meant a country with which we did not have undue trouble, while to Stalin "a friendly neighbor" meant a country which he dominated and controlled.

I used to discuss this and other problems with my deputy, George Kennan, for whose knowledge and experience I had great respect. It had taken Hopkins' help and nine months' effort on my part to pry him away from other duties for assignment in Moscow.

In my cables to Washington I referred several times to the problem of the meaning of words; for example on September 20, 1944, I said: "The Russians have in mind something quite different from what we would mean when they insist on having 'friendly governments' in their neighboring countries. . . . To put it in terms that we would understand, I believe that it is their intention to have a positive sphere of influence over their western neighbors and the Balkan countries. . . . It may be argued that the affairs of this area need not concern American interests. However, what frightens me is this: when a country, by strong-arm methods but under the guise of security, begins to extend its influence beyond its borders, it is difficult to see how a line can be drawn. Once the policy is accepted that the U.S.S.R. has a right to penetrate its immediate neighbors for security, penetration of the next immediate neighbors becomes equally logical at a certain time. . . ."

But Stalin did agree at Yalta to set up an interim government in Poland, bringing in the London Poles, the free Poles from within Poland, together with the Lublin Poles, and holding "free and unfettered" elections. In addition, he agreed to the comprehensive Declaration on Liberated Europe—that all the other nations of Eastern Europe would

have the right to hold free elections, that the three governments would work together to see that they were carried out
and that all non-Fascist democratic parties had the right to
participate. This was all spelled out. There was a further
agreement about the Far East, which I will refer to later.

Roosevelt and Churchill came back from Yalta feeling
that they had reached agreements. Roosevelt went to the
Congress and Churchill to the Parliament and spoke optimistically about the agreements.

Churchill reported to the House of Commons that, "The
Crimean Conference leaves the Allies more closely united than
before, both in the military and the political sphere." On Poland he added, "Most solemn declarations have been made by
Marshal Stalin and the Soviet Union that the sovereign independence of Poland is to be maintained, and this decision is
now joined in both by Great Britain and the United States."
Roosevelt in his speech to a joint session of both Houses of the
Congress declared, "One outstanding example of joint action
by the three major Allied powers in the liberated areas was the
solution reached on Poland." He concluded by emphasizing
the importance he placed on the United Nations as finding
". . . a common ground for peace. It ought to spell the end of
the system of unilateral action, the exclusive alliances, the
spheres of influence, the balances of power, and all the other
expedients that have . . . always failed."

There has grown a myth about Yalta that somehow or
other Roosevelt and Churchill sold out Eastern Europe to
Stalin. That wasn't true at all. I can't imagine why Stalin
went to such extreme lengths in breaking the Yalta agreements if it had been true that they were so much to his
advantage. It was agreed that the people in these countries

were to decide on their own governments through free elections. But Stalin didn't permit it.

One wonders why he broke his agreement on Poland so soon. It's rather hard to guess. Personally, I think one of the reasons was that Bierut, the leading member of the Lublin Polish government—the Communist government—was in Moscow on Stalin's return from Yalta. He may have told Stalin that if he carried out his plan for free elections, Bierut and his comrades couldn't deliver Poland. Stalin had the idea that the Red Army would be accepted as a liberating army. In fact, he told me so. In this regard, perhaps the Communist partisans had reported too optimistically to Moscow. At any rate I think the Kremlin leaders were awfully hurt when they found that the Red Army was looked upon by the Poles, the Romanians, and others as a new invading force.

In addition, there appeared to be two schools of thought in the Kremlin hierarchy—the Politburo itself. One is apt to think of the Communist government as one single brain; it isn't. It is made up of men with sometimes differing views; this was true even under Stalin. I was conscious of the fact that members of Politburo even during the war had different views on different subjects. Let me quickly say that there was free discussion in the Politburo on *new* subjects only. On anything Stalin had decided, that was it. That couldn't be questioned. I think it is fair to say that in these discussions about new matters, Stalin listened, smoked his pipe, and walked up and down the room. Then, when he had heard enough, he said, "This is what we are going to do." If anyone left the room with a shrug of his shoulders, he might find himself on the way to Siberia the next afternoon. That may be somewhat of an exaggeration, but I think it's pretty nearly right.

In any event, I feel sure that there was a difference of opinion as to whether it would be wise for the Soviet Union in the immediate postwar period to soft-pedal Communist expansion for a time and continue to collaborate with the Western Allies to get the value of loans and trade, technical assistance, and other cooperation for the terrific job of reconstruction they faced; or whether they should push ahead and use the extraordinary opportunities in the dislocations in Europe and elsewhere to extend Communist control. Stalin once told me, "Communism breeds in the cesspools of capitalists." In this sense, Europe looked as if it were going to be in a mire.

I was so concerned about this that in early 1945, I sent messages about the need to help Western Europe, urging that the recovery of Europe would require much more than most people thought. I said that UNRRA would not be enough, food would not be enough. We would have to supply working capital and raw materials to get trade going again. Imports would be needed for raw materials for industrial production as well as for reconstruction. Without that, there would be vast unemployment and misery, in which the Communists might well take over.

I believe that Stalin hoped to get to the Atlantic, and that was perhaps the reason why he didn't carry out the Yalta agreements. The prospects for Communist takeover simply looked too good.

He said a number of things on different occasions, some of them contradictory, and it is hard to know what he had in mind. After Teheran he sent President Roosevelt a telegram in which, among other things, he said, "Now it is assured that our people will act together, jointly and in friendship, both at the present time and after the completion of the war." This is only one of the many expressions of that kind which gave some indication that he had in mind post-war cooperation. But that didn't happen. Roosevelt died, and I know that before he died he realized that his hopes had not been fully achieved; he knew Stalin had already broken some of the Yalta agreements. I know that from the tele-grams I received from him to deliver to Stalin and also from some of the people who talked to him just before his death.

These included Senator Vandenberg, Anne O'Hare Mc-Cormick, Herbert Bayard Swope, and Anna Rosenberg Hoffman.[3]

For example, on April 1, eleven days before his death, Roosevelt sent this message for me to transmit to Stalin:

"I cannot conceal from you the concern with which I view the developments of events of mutual interest since our fruitful meeting at Yalta. The decisions we reached there were good ones and have for the most part been welcomed with enthusi-asm by the peoples of the world who saw in our ability to find a common basis of understanding the best pledge for a secure and peaceful world after this war. . . . So far there has been a discouraging lack of progress made in the carrying out, which the world expects, of the political decisions which we reached at the conference particularly those relating to the Polish ques-tion. . . .

[3] Mrs. Hoffman wrote me a letter some years later describing her con-versation with Roosevelt on March 24, 1945, his last day in Washington:

The President was in his wheel chair as we left the room, and both Mrs. Roosevelt and I walked at his side. He was given a message which I learned later was a cable from you which had been decoded. He read it and became quite angry. He banged his fists on the arms of his wheel chair and said, "Averell is right; we can't do business with Stalin. He has broken every one of the promises he made at Yalta." He was very upset and continued in the same vein on the subject.

These were his exact words. I remembered them and verified them with Mrs. Roosevelt not too long before her death.

"I must make it quite plain to you that any such solution which would result in a thinly disguised continuance of the present Warsaw regime would be unacceptable and would cause the people of the United States to regard the Yalta agreement as having failed."

The news of President Roosevelt's death reached us in Moscow in the late evening because of the nine hours difference in time. It came as an immense shock to Russians and Americans alike. Molotov called on me at Spaso House at once to express the condolences of Stalin and the Soviet government. His attitude appeared to be one of bewilderment and concern about the significance of this tragic event. He indicated that Stalin wished to see me, and it was arranged that I would call on him the next day.

When I saw Stalin he appeared deeply shaken and more disturbed than I had ever seen him. He held my hand for some time. He asked about President Truman and I assured him that President Truman would carry out Roosevelt's policies, but I added that the world would be disturbed and that I believed he could take action which would help give confidence that the allies would continue in close collaboration. When he asked what I had in mind, I suggested that it would be impressive if he were to send Foreign Minister Molotov, rather than his deputy, Vishinsky, to the United Nations Conference. Molotov demurred and whispered something in Stalin's ear that I couldn't get. Stalin, however, overruled him and said Molotov would go. Stalin stated, "President Roosevelt has died but his cause must live on. We shall support President Truman with our forces and all our will." He asked me to tell this to President Truman on my return to Washington.

I left Moscow three days later. I felt that I had to see President Truman as soon as possible in order to give him as accurate a picture as possible of our relations with the Soviet Union. I wanted to be sure that he understood that Stalin was already failing to keep his Yalta commitment. Much to my surprise, when I saw President Truman I found that he had already read all the telegrams between Washington and Moscow and had a clear understanding of the problems we faced. For the first time I learned how avid a reader President Truman was. This was one of the reasons he was able to take on so rapidly the immense problems he had to deal with at that time. He wanted to know what I believed Roosevelt had in mind. He grasped the importance of the Polish problem and took the opportunity of Molotov's call on him to impress on him bluntly, perhaps too bluntly, the United States' insistence that the Yalta agreement be carried out.

Our differences with the Soviet Union were becoming increasingly acute, and I was worried that the Kremlin might get the idea that it was a change of American personality rather than their own intransigence that was the cause. Chip Bohlen and I got the idea that it would be a good thing for Harry Hopkins to go to Moscow and talk with Stalin to demonstrate the continuity of policy. I knew that Stalin recognized Hopkins as the closest of Roosevelt's advisers, and also that he had an unusual regard for Hopkins because he had been the first of the Western Allies to come to Moscow after the Nazi attack. I proposed it to the President, and he agreed.

Although Hopkins was seriously ill, he immediately responded to President Truman's request and came to Moscow before the end of May, shortly after my own return. He had several cordial talks with Stalin and felt that he had convinced Stalin of the need to deal fairly with the Poles. Unhappily, Stalin failed again to carry out fully what Hopkins thought had been agreed on. However, in the atmosphere of Hopkins' visit we were able to get Stalin to agree about several fundamental differences we were having in San Francisco over United Nations procedures.

The two fundamental differences that Secretary of State Stettinius referred to us in Moscow had already been in dispute while I was in San Francisco. Some of us had recommended that they were so vital that if the Soviets did not give in on both, we should break and go ahead without them in an international organization of like-minded nations. We could then raise our sights and have more ambitious objectives. Stettinius stood firm, and one of these issues was referred to us while Hopkins was still in Moscow. With Hopkins' support, I discussed it with Stalin, and he finally agreed with our position, overruling Molotov. The second came after Hopkins left. I argued it out with Molotov, requesting a meeting with Stalin if he didn't agree. This time Molotov, after consulting Stalin, informed me Stalin had accepted our draft.

Looking back, it seems even clearer today than in 1945 that if we had not stood firm on these two procedural questions, the United Nations would have been a far less effective organization. The first question related to voting procedure in the Security Council on whether to consider complaints brought to it by a member country. The Soviets wanted these to be regarded as substantive questions to which the veto would apply. We insisted that they be regarded as procedural questions which could be decided by seven affirmative votes out of the eleven members. If the Soviets could have blocked the Security Council from considering any question, the Council would have become impotent.

The second question related to the powers of the Assembly. The Soviets wanted to give the Security Council authority to fix the agenda for the Assembly, and no question could be considered by the Assembly that was not on this agenda. Obviously this control of the Assembly by the Security Council, where the Soviet veto applied, would have made that body of insignificant importance.

I believe these were the two last important differences whose settlement cleared the way for the launching of the United Nations.

While I was home, I did spend several weeks in San Francisco during the United Nations Conference. At the request of Ed Stettinius, the Secretary of State, I had three off-the-record talks with editors, columnists, and reporters to give them some background on our growing problems with the Soviet government. I told them we would have real difficulties with the Soviet Union in the postwar period. This came as a great shock to many of them. At one meeting, I explained that our objectives and the Kremlin objectives were irreconcilable; they wanted to communize the world, and we wanted a free world. But I added that we would have to find ways to compose our differences if we were to live in peace on this small planet. Two men were so shocked that they got up and left. Some of the press at that time criticized me for being so unkind to what were then known as "our gallant allies," and some even suggested that I should be recalled as Ambassador. It was one of the few times in my experience that members of the press have broken the confidence of an off-the-record talk.

People ask when and why I became convinced we would have difficulties with the Soviets. This judgment developed over a period of time.

For instance, in a cable of September 9, 1944, I reported to Hopkins to show the President:

Our relations with the Soviets now that the end of the war is in sight have taken a startling turn evident during the last two months. The Soviets have held up our requests with complete indifference to our interests and have shown an unwillingness even to discuss pressing problems. . . .

Since early in the year I have been conscious of a division among Stalin's advisers on the question of cooperation with us. My feeling now is that those who oppose the kind of cooperation we expect have recently been getting their way and the policy appears to be crystallizing to force us and the British to accept all Soviet policies backed by the strength and prestige of the Red Army. . . .

We can, I am convinced, divert this trend, but only if we change materially our policy toward the Soviet Government. I have evidence that they have misinterpreted our general attitude toward them as an acceptance of their policies and a sign of weakness. . . .

The time has come when we must make clear what we expect of the Soviets as the price of our goodwill. There is every indication that unless we take issue with the present policy the Soviet Union will become a world bully wherever their interests are involved. . . .

I am disappointed but not discouraged. This job of getting the Soviet Government to play a decent role in international affairs is, however, going to be more difficult than we had hoped.

I found out later that this telegram was read by a number of senior officials in State, War, and Navy.

A talk I had with Stalin at Potsdam in July 1945 is illuminating. The first time I saw him at the conference I went up to him and said that it must be very gratifying for him to be in Berlin, after all the struggle and the tragedy. He hesitated a moment and then replied, "Czar Alexander got to Paris." It didn't need much of a clairvoyant to guess what was in his mind.

I don't think there is any doubt that, with the strong Communist Parties both in Italy and in France, he would have extended his domination to the Atlantic, if we had not acted to frustrate it. In all probability, the Communist leaders in those countries had reported to Moscow that they could take over, and I think they would have succeeded if we had not helped Western Europe to recover. Some of Western Europe would have had Communist governments under the control of Moscow. One doesn't know what the rest of Europe would have been like, but perhaps some countries would have been something less independent than Finland and allowed to be cautiously neutral at the grace of Moscow.

But that isn't what happened. I know that some young people think that everything that has been done before them wasn't just right, but we did have a fairly glorious period, perhaps the most creative period in American foreign policy, immediately after the war. It was due to the leadership of President Truman and the effective cooperation of Senator Vandenberg, the Republican Senator from Michigan, who was then Chairman of the Foreign Relations Committee. The undertakings included aid to Greece, which was under Communist attack, and Turkey, which was threatened at that time; the Marshall Plan, which was an extraordinarily ambitious and successful venture in cooperation; and that led to NATO. These things developed one from the other.

Public opinion in the West was deeply disturbed by the Czech coup of March 1948 and then the Berlin blockade three months later.

The Soviet pressure on Turkey began as early as October 1945. The Soviets demanded not only a naval base at the Dardanelles but the "return" of the two eastern Turkish provinces to Russia. The tenuous claim was based on the fact that these territories had once been controlled by czarist Russia. The annexation of these two provinces would have brought the Soviet border over the mountains into the plains, obviously putting the rest of Turkey in a most indefensible position. But Turkey flatly rejected the Soviet demands. The Turkish Ambassador, Sarper, told me of his talk with the Soviet Foreign Office. When he had stated the Turkish position, the Soviet asked whether the Ambassador understood the grave consequences of such an unfriendly attitude toward their strong neighbor. Ambassador Sarper replied: "I don't know what you mean by grave consequences, but if you mean war, we are ready to fight." Turkey was the first of the independent nations to defy Soviet aggression.

In February 1947 we were faced with the announcement by the British that they had to pull out of Greece, since they could no longer afford the cost. The United States was faced with the decision whether to let Greece fall under Communist control or to respond to the Greek government's request for assistance. The Greeks were fighting a Communist insurgency supported by her Communist neighbors to the north. President Truman's decision to aid Greece and Turkey was a revolutionary change in American foreign policy. In this decision Dean Acheson, then Under Secretary of State, played a vital role. This was the first time we took a major responsibility during peacetime in Europe. The Marshall Plan, although far more massive, was a logical sequel to this decision. President Truman's initiatives were in marked contrast to our retreat into isolationism after World War I.

I was involved in the Marshall Plan, in charge of operations in Europe for more than two years. This was a European effort, with United States help. By the way, I should recall that General Marshall's offer of aid was made to all of Europe, including Russia and Eastern Europe. In fact, Molotov came to the meeting of Foreign Ministers of the European countries called in Paris in July 1947 to consider Marshall's offer with a staff of sixty, including senior economists. However, he demanded that each country act independently. He wanted the European nations to reply to the United States along these lines, "Tell us how much money you will give us, and we will divide it on the basis of those who suffered most will get the most. Then each country will look after its own recovery." But Marshall's proposal was that the European countries should cooperate together in a mutual recovery program. Bevin and Bidault, the British and French Foreign Ministers, stood firm for the cooperative concept, and Molotov left in a huff. The Czechs and the Poles had wanted to join the Marshall Plan, but the Kremlin ordered them not to do so.

At that time the Soviets organized the Cominform and declared war on the Marshall Plan, calling it an "American imperialist plot to subjugate Western Europe." Needless to say, that was just exactly the reverse of what we wanted. We wanted a strong, united and independent Europe. Everything that we did was to minimize our role and maximize the cooperative effort of the Europeans. "Self-help and mutual aid" was the slogan. It was amazingly successful—

a spirit of cooperation and unity developed within Europe which had never before existed. They abandoned some of the restrictive business and labor practices of the intra-war years and accepted the necessity of an expanding economy as the basis for a rising standard of living.

As an international banker I had seen the difficult economic position of Europe during the intra-war period. I still vividly recall a discussion I had with some of the leading European bankers and industrialists in Paris in 1927. This was at an informal dinner during a meeting of the Executive Committee of the International Chamber of Commerce. I raised the question of why, while Europe was in a period of stagnation with high unemployment, we in the United States were prosperous with expanding production. There was unanimous agreement that the primary reason was that we had a continent of free trade, whereas in Europe there were restrictive trade barriers between each of the countries. I asked them why, if that were true, they didn't do something about breaking down these barriers. They replied again unanimously that that was impossible unless there were mutual security arrangements among the European countries. Each country at that time had its own military forces and therefore wanted to be as autarchic as possible so as to supply its military needs—from heavy steel castings for guns to buttons for uniforms.

My experiences during this period convinced me that in the postwar years a combined security arrangement such as NATO was essential to end the military pressures for autarchy and permit economic integration.

Now, Western Europe is more vital and dynamic than ever. When De Gaulle was in control, France was, perhaps, a little too nationalistic. But today the Europeans are again moving toward greater integration and closer cooperation. This was part of the objective of the Congress, and certainly of President Truman in initiating the Marshall Plan.

The Congress declared in the preamble of the enabling legislation for the Marshall Plan—the Economic Cooperation Act of 1948:

> Mindful of the advantages which the United States has enjoyed through the existence of a large domestic market with no internal trade barriers, and believing that similar advantages can accrue to the countries of Europe, it is declared to be the policy of the people of the United States to encourage these countries through joint organization to exert sustained common efforts . . . which will speedily achieve that economic cooperation in Europe which is essential for lasting peace and prosperity.

In the 1949 Act, emphasis was added regarding integration:

> It is further declared to be the policy of the people of the United States to encourage the unification of Europe. . . .

The Berlin blockade in June of 1948 was a startling event and led to the pressure for NATO. You have to remember that never in history has a nation destroyed its armed strength as rapidly as we did after the Second World War. The demand for bringing the boys home was irresistible. No one was to blame; it was the deep desire of the American people. We thought we had won the war and everyone in the world would want peace. We had the strongest military force in being at the end of the war, but after the Japanese surrendered, it was dissipated. The Russians didn't do that. They strengthened their forces. They developed new weapons. We in Moscow reported to Washington in late 1945 evidence which indicated that Soviet research expenditure was being doubled, that production of certain new weapons and military equipment was continuing at wartime levels, and that combat training for the Red Army was being emphasized.

Although for a time we had a monopoly in nuclear weapons, Stalin ordered the highest priority be given to developing nuclear capability. Much to the surprise of most people at the time, the Soviets exploded their first nuclear device in September 1949.[4]

The Berlin blockade was countered not by direct force. There has been a lot of argument about that at the time and since. People can argue whether Truman's decision was right or wrong—whether to try to drive our forces through and threaten a nuclear attack, or whether to supply Berlin by airlift. In any event, the least provocative of these responses —the airlift—was chosen, and with full British cooperation it was successful. The Soviets lifted the blockade a year later.

We have had difficulty over Berlin ever since, sometimes more dangerous than others. Of course, one can criticize the arrangements which made Berlin the capital of occupied Germany. Frankly, Ben Cohen[5] and I favored at the time a capital in a new location, where the three zones came together, just north of Magdeburg. I was influenced in part by the appalling way in which the Soviets had stripped Berlin of most everything they could take out, between V-E Day and the Potsdam meeting. The factories, particularly, were emp-

---

[4] Later the fact that Dr. Klaus Fuchs had treacherously passed valuable nuclear information to the Soviet was exposed. This information undoubtedly contributed to the rapid development.

[5] Benjamin V. Cohen, then serving as assistant to Secretary of State Byrnes.

tied of all machinery and machine tools. But these arrangements had been made by the European Advisory Commission in London. They had been accepted by the three Allies and would have been pretty hard to change at Potsdam.

Sometimes I have thought our presence in Berlin was of great value. Other times I have wondered if it was worthwhile. These are things that historians can argue about. But we are there in West Berlin, and the division of Germany continues along the line of the Soviet occupational zone.

Some think that General Eisenhower should have taken Berlin, but if he had done that, our Third Army wouldn't have been in Austria, and Austria, which is a free and independent country, probably would have been occupied largely by the Red Army and might have been turned into a satellite.

These are all questions which one can weigh. It is hard to say what might have been done. If one objective had been gained, something else would have been lost. I think by and large with the Soviet recalcitrance it would have made very little difference.

Some people have even argued that if General Eisenhower had liberated Prague somehow or other Czechoslovakia would be free today. That's nonsense! The Czech government under President Benes was set up under an agreement in Moscow, negotiated by Benes with Czech party leaders, including the Communists. This government returned to Czechoslovakia from the East, as the Red Army, joined with four or five Czech divisions, advanced. Under the agreement Benes had to take Communists into the government.

I had several talks with Benes when he came to Moscow from London in March 1945 before returning to Czechoslovakia. He told me that he was not too well satisfied with the composition of the new government, but he added, "It might have been worse." Benes was confident he could control the situation in Czechoslovakia as he believed the people would support him. He told me that Stalin had assured him that the Soviets would not interfere in Czech internal affairs.

Unfortunately, Benes was ill in March 1948 when the coup took place. Of course, the Red Army had long since retired. It had withdrawn from Czechoslovakia more than two years earlier. Our troops had also withdrawn long before, so nothing we did in 1945 would have affected the outcome. Whether or not it would have been different if Benes had been well and vigorous, and whether he could have held his own, I don't know. But the Communist coup was successful without the participation of the Red Army, but undoubtedly with Moscow's collusion.

I had long talks with Jan Masaryk in San Francisco in May 1945. He was Benes' Foreign Minister. He told me I must understand that in the United Nations he would have to vote with Molotov. The Soviets were insisting that the Czech government support them in foreign policy. In return, he thought they would have a free hand at home. Unfortunately, it did not work out that way, and Masaryk himself came to a violent end in March 1948.

The Truman period was an exciting period. President Truman was a man of great determination. He was very humble at the start. He said he had not been elected; Roosevelt had been elected, and it was his responsibility to carry out Roosevelt's policies. He did the best he could. Very early he showed that he recognized the unique problems facing the United States in the world, and he had the extraordinary courage to undertake new policies and programs. And I think they were extraordinarily successful.

President Truman proposed in January 1949 the Point Four Program, announcing that since science and technology had developed to such a point that the old enemies of mankind—hunger, misery, poverty, and disease—could be overcome, it was the obligation of the United States and other more technologically advanced nations to help. That concept has moved ahead. There have been some outstanding successes in some ways and in some countries—some disappointments in others. Unfortunately, our development assistance is in rather a low state today—one of the casualties of Vietnam.

There have been lasting constructive results from the Truman period. Germany has revived and has become a strong ally; Japan has revived and is becoming a strong partner. Western Europe is more productive and united than ever. Other countries have made progress as well and are on their way to sustained economic development, for example in Asia, Korea, and Taiwan, and in Latin America, Mexico, Venezuela, and Colombia. There have been disappointments, of course. The developing countries as a whole have not been able to advance as rapidly as had been hoped, and the gap between them and the industrial nations has widened.

China was an enigma. Roosevelt first of all wanted to get the Soviet Union into the war against Japan. There was never any doubt in my mind that Stalin would attack Japan when it suited him. We could not have kept him out. The question was whether that would be soon enough to do us good. Our Chiefs of Staff estimated that it would take eighteen months after the fall of Germany to defeat the Japanese and would require an amphibious landing on the plains of Tokyo. American casualties were estimated to run up near a million with perhaps a couple of hundred thousand killed. This was a grim prospect to President Roosevelt. Yet, if the Russians attacked the Japanese Kwangtung Army in

Manchuria, the Japanese strength to defend the home islands would be reduced. President Roosevelt had a deep sense of responsibility to protect American lives, and it was hoped that possibly, with Russia in the war and with American use of Soviet airfields in Siberia, we could bring Japan to surrender without invasion. Therefore, Soviet intervention seemed of vital importance.

It didn't turn out to be important because, unexpectedly, the nuclear bomb became operative and events moved so rapidly. At Yalta, when plans about Soviet entry into the war against Japan were agreed to, the nuclear bomb had not yet been completed, and nobody knew whether it would work. Even five months later at Potsdam, after the first test explosion took place, one of the most distinguished Navy officers bet an apple that it would not go off as a bomb. Of course, after things happen they seem so easy and so obvious that people say, "Why didn't you think of this at the time?"

Apart from Soviet entry into the war, Roosevelt also wanted to get Stalin to accept Chiang Kai-shek's Nationalist government as the government of China. And that, too, was part of the agreements reached at Yalta about the Far East. This was formalized in a treaty negotiated by T. V. Soong, Premier of the Nationalist government, with Stalin six months later. During these negotiations in Moscow I saw T. V. Soong almost every day. He was finally well satisfied, and in fact the world applauded the agreement.

For example, *Life* magazine declared in an editorial at the time: "Twelve days after Japan gave up there was announced in Moscow and Chungking an agreement which was as great a victory for common sense as the defeat of Japan was for armed might. The Soong-Stalin treaties contain less ammunition for pessimists than any diplomatic event of the last 20 years. The signatures of two men have done as much to assure peace as all our flying fortresses. . . .

"Two strong and subtle men, both revolutionaries since youth, sat down in Moscow and discovered that each needed and wanted a long peace to complete his particular revolution. So they negotiated out every major issue between Russia and China. . . .

"Peace, lively but genuine peace, is therefore the outlook."

There were certain concessions to the Russians related to the railroads and ports in Manchuria for a thirty-year period, but the important point for Chiang was that the Soviets accepted Chinese sovereignty over the area. Some of us had been concerned when the Russians got into Manchuria they would establish a "Manchurian People's Republic" just as they had the Mongolian People's Republic. The fact that the Soviets accepted Chinese sovereignty was the thing that impressed Chiang.

Curiously, Stalin did not have much respect for Mao Tse-tung. During the war he spoke about him several times, and at one time he called him a "margarine Communist." That created a great deal of puzzlement in Washington. Some didn't know what it means. It would be entirely clear to any dairy farmer what he meant—a fake, not a real product. I gained the impression from several of my talks with Stalin that he was not keen to support Mao Tse-tung in China and that, perhaps, he wanted to see a new group more amenable to Moscow, take over the Chinese Communist Party before he gave his full support.

After the war, in January 1946, he told me that he had "poor contacts with the Communists." He said that the Soviet government's "three representatives in Yenan had been recalled" and that the Soviet influence with the Chinese Communists was not great. I think there is other evidence to that effect. For example, the Red Army not only stripped Manchuria of its industrial machinery for use in the Soviet Union but also blew up facilities such as blast furnaces. However, the Mao Communists were stronger than Stalin thought, and Chiang was weaker. As events developed, Chiang's forces collapsed in 1949, and he was driven out of mainland China.

Some people have said, "We lost China." It just happens that we never owned China. Whatever we had done in China over the years had had only a limited impact. And although it is unfortunate that a government friendly to us did not survive, we could not have involved ourselves in a major war at that time in China. President Truman, in spite of all the initiatives we had taken in other parts of the world, was wise enough to exercise restraint and not become involved in a civil war in mainland China.[6]

So not all the postwar developments were favorable. Some of them did not go as well as we had hoped they might.

Looking back, we can also consider what might have been done about Korea. We had taken our troops out in the summer of 1949. The North Koreans attacked South Korea in June 1950. There is no doubt in my mind that Stalin organized the North Korean force, trained and armed them. Officers and men of Korean descent living in Siberia who had fought in the Red Army were sent back to join the North Korean Army.

I am convinced Stalin directed the attack on South Korea and did not think that we would intervene except to protest to the United Nations. Stalin had hoped, I believe, at the end of the war to get a zone of occupation in Japan as in

[6] See page 65 for more on postwar China.

Germany, or at least Soviet troops occupying the island of Hokkaido under General MacArthur as Supreme Allied Commander. When this did not materialize, Stalin may have begun to consider attempting to get control of all of Korea through the "friendly" Communist North Korean government as a means of exerting greater influence on Japan. The port of Pusan in southern Korea is only about 125 miles from Japan's main island, Honshu, and only 40 miles from the strategic island, Tsushima, in the Korean Straits. He did not expect us to intervene militarily but only to protest in the United Nations. Evidence we have tends to confirm Soviet involvement—the speed with which Soviet propaganda organs supported the North Koreans—the very day of the attack, and the considerable number of Russian military advisers in North Korea at that time.

President Truman faced a difficult decision—whether to let Korea collapse or try to defend it with our limited military resources at the time. Korea was a country that had been divided in 1945 as a result of arrangements to facilitate the acceptance of Japanese surrender there. The 38th Parallel had been proposed by our military and the Soviets agreed to it. The Red Army stopped its advance into Korea at that parallel some weeks before we landed and came up from the south. We later tried unsuccessfully to work out an arrangement which would permit unification of the country. Korea had been discussed at Yalta in private talks between Roosevelt and Stalin. They agreed that Korea should become a united, independent country. Roosevelt suggested a trusteeship under the United Nations for a limited number of years so that the Koreans could develop their own governmental procedures. But I doubt that the South Koreans would have had any part of a trusteeship. They wanted to rule themselves at once and were determined to. As in other cases, the Soviets refused to agree to the unification of the two areas.

When President Truman decided to defend South Korea, we obtained full United Nations support for every move. Military units were sent from a number of United Nations countries, and General MacArthur was designated the United Nations Commander-in-Chief.

In retrospect, a mistake was perhaps made in crossing the 38th Parallel after the success of the Inchon landing in September 1950. However, the rout of the North Koreans was so complete that it would have been hard to stop efforts to destroy their retreating forces. Clearly it was a tragic mistake that we did not stop at a line at the neck just north of Pyongyang. The British and others recommended this.

MacArthur was ordered not to permit any of his forces other than the South Koreans to go north of the Chungjo-Yongwon-Hungnam line. Although he had agreed to these orders, he disobeyed them and sent American forces north toward the Yalu River. He was convinced that his only problem was to complete destruction of the North Korean armies and had sent a message to the Joint Chiefs that he had lifted the restrictions "as a matter of military necessity." Although Truman had announced that it was his understanding that only Korean troops would approach the northern border, MacArthur stated to the press that "the mission of the United Nations Force is to clear Korea." MacArthur was so convinced that the Chinese would not intervene that he recklessly divided his forces under two field commanders and left a gap between them.

Truman had gone all the way out to Wake Island in October 1950 to see him and warn him to avoid actions which would get us involved with the Chinese. Unfortunately, he didn't follow this advice. He was quite sure. I can still vividly recall his telling Mr. Truman in his deep, dramatic voice that he knew the Chinese; that they would never attack, but should they attack, it would be "the greatest slaughter."

This wasn't what happened. The Chinese attacked and drove our forces so far back into South Korea that General MacArthur began to consider evacuation. At this point General Walker was killed in a Jeep accident, and General Matthew Ridgway became field commander in his place. With a remarkable display of leadership, he rallied our forces and turned the tide of battle. General Ridgway's performance was one of the most brilliant in our military history. He drove the Chinese back to the 38th Parallel. Again there was a question of advancing into North Korea, but Truman decided this time to stop at about the 38th Parallel. I have no doubt that this decision was right. We had succeeded in our basic objective of preventing the North from taking over South Korea.

Some people talk about winning or not winning a limited war. It's a lot of nonsense. You don't "win" a limited war; you try to achieve your objective. In Korea our original objective was to stop and throw back the attack from the North—and we achieved that objective. The South Koreans are today a vigorous, independent country and have done extraordinarily well in the development of their own resources. They are able to take care of themselves, although they still need help in military equipment and in the stationing of a limited number of United States troops if another attack is to be deterred.

Stalin died shortly after Truman left office in 1953, and new leaders took over in both Washington and Moscow. And now again I was on the side lines, and as a back seat driver

I thought many things could have been done differently during that period.

Dulles played a leading role in shaping the Eisenhower administration's foreign policy. To me the first major mistake was "unleashing" Chiang. Undoubtedly Senator Knowland (Republican leader of the Senate) and the China lobby influenced this decision. Truman had been guarded in his relations with Chiang. He clearly understood that there was no chance for Chiang to return to the mainland but that Chiang might try to provoke an incident involving us in war with Red China through which he might attempt to regain power.

This decision to "unleash" Chiang had far-reaching effects. Not only did it lead to crises with Red China, but it began to undermine the respect that many people throughout the world had for the wisdom of American leadership.

Also, during the 1952 campaign Dulles had proposed his "liberation" policy for the countries of Eastern Europe. I debated this policy with him face-to-face on several occasions during that campaign. I pointed out the danger of encouraging the people in those countries to revolt when we had no feasible way to come to their assistance. I said that if this policy was announced it would lead to the death of many brave patriots.

After the 1956 Hungarian uprising, suppressed by the Red Army, thirty to forty thousand Hungarian refugees were admitted into the United States. I was then Governor of New York and we helped settle about one third of them in the State. I saw many of the young men and women who had taken part in this uprising. All of them told me they had believed we would come to their assistance.

In 1956 Dulles encouraged Nasser to believe we would help finance the Aswan Dam. Regardless of the reasons for withdrawing from the project, the manner in which Dulles did it was so curt and insulting that it contributed to Nasser's turning against us and his growing reliance on the Soviet Union.

Perhaps Dulles' most damaging statement affecting our relations with the uncommitted nations was his pronouncement that he considered neutrality morally wrong. This attitude was incredible since the United States itself had been neutral for most of its life as a nation. He took the position that Communism was evil and that countries were either for us or against us in our struggle with it.

In addition, Dulles' expounding of the theory of "brinkmanship" and "massive retaliation" further brought into question the soundness of our policies.

In that period I was also concerned over Dulles' policies of organizing military alliances with weaker countries around the perimeter of Russia and China—SEATO and CENTO. I felt that the net effect would be provocative and not add to our security or that of the countries involved.

However, throughout this period President Eisenhower's warm personality and his personal contacts with foreign leaders offset to some extent the concern that was developing over our policies. I was greatly heartened to hear favorable reports of President Eisenhower's talks with Chairman Khrushchev at Camp David in the fall of 1959. A summit conference was arranged in Paris the following May, and it was generally understood that President Eisenhower would pay a return visit to the Soviet Union shortly thereafter. Knowing the enormous respect the Russian people had for General Eisenhower as a war hero, I believed his visit would be of profound and lasting importance. He had come to Moscow in July 1945 and was given a hero's welcome. He and Marshal Zhukov had attended a soccer game at the enormous Dynamo stadium, and they were introduced during the intermission. The cheers of the crowd "raised the sky" when the two war leaders stood up with their arms around each others' shoulders. I had high hopes that Eisenhower's visit in 1960 would have created such widespread good will among the Russian people that it could not help affecting the Kremlin leadership in dealing with the issues between us.

The U-2 incident killed all this, and the cold war was again in the deep freeze. The undertaking of that flight at that time was an unwarranted risk.

Nevertheless, there were a number of constructive achievements during the Eisenhower administration. NATO was strengthened, and the policy of bringing West Germany into the alliance was continued. An armistice was agreed to in Korea in July 1953, although a real peace was not achieved. The settlement of Trieste between Italy and Yugoslavia was brought about. Of great significance was the agreement reached for the independence and neutrality of Austria in 1955. There was a continuation and expansion of some programs, including foreign aid, and during the closing months of the Administration, increased attention was given to cooperation in Latin America, a forerunner to President Kennedy's Alliance for Progress.

In 1959 I got to know Khrushchev quite well. I had several talks with him in Moscow, one of them lasting ten hours, and several months later he came to my home in New York. Then I invited some thirty-five leading bankers and businessmen to meet him. When I introduced them to him he replied, "You rule America. You are the ruling circle."

I never realized that you could learn so much about a man in one long session. I went to his office in the Kremlin at one o'clock and talked for a couple of hours. Then we drove to his country dacha were we walked in the garden and started dinner at four-thirty. I stayed on until eleven o'clock. Mikoyan joined us, as did Gromyko and Koslov, who Khrushchev told me was going to succeed him. We talked about almost everything.

He was rough and tough about some things and affable and amusing about others. He declared with vehemence, "We are determined to liquidate your rights in West Berlin." He added threateningly, "Your generals talk of tanks and guns defending your Berlin position. Your tanks would burn and the missiles would fly." When I said I couldn't believe he really would provoke war with us, he backed away saying, "We don't want war over Berlin."

In speaking of Stalin he said, "We don't consider Stalin without blame." He told me that during Stalin's later years he had become more aloof and more suspicious. He trusted no one. Khrushchev said that when he and his colleagues were called to his office, they didn't know when they would see their families again. He explained that people couldn't work in that kind of an atmosphere. I said I could understand that. Khrushchev added that when Stalin died, they got together and agreed that no one man would have complete control again. However, he said they had "a little trouble" with one man, Beria, head of the secret police. "He was a little overly ambitious."

You remember they shot him—but he was the last man they have had to shoot. Since then they have retired a number of their senior Kremlin people—Malenkov, Molotov, Bulganin, more recently Mikoyan and then Khrushchev himself—and all of them are living quite comfortably. I don't know if they are living happily, but they are living comfortably, with a dacha in the country. The Soviets have become more civilized in the succession to power and in retiring voluntarily or involuntarily those who held it.

There were real changes from Stalin to Khrushchev. The knock on the door at midnight was ended. People were no longer dragged out of their beds, never to be heard of again. And there is today a semblance of a trial—not what we would approve of—but an improvement over the past. There is still an active secret police, but it is no longer controlled by the whim of one man. Of course, they still exercise strict discipline of public expression critical of the system in a manner repugnant to us.

We had a number of serious and dangerous confrontations with Khrushchev. He was determined that East Germany would be accepted. He was determined to force a decision in Germany to take over Berlin. On the other hand, there are a number of things which he did which were constructive. He permitted Austria to regain its independence. He settled Trieste. And then he agreed to the Limited Nuclear Test Ban Treaty.

President Kennedy's inaugural speech created intense interest and high expectation around the world about the new Administration. This was impressed on me by the manner in which I was received when at the President's request I visited a number of countries in Europe, the Middle East and Asia several weeks later, and talked with the heads of governments. I spent an evening with Macmillan in London. In Paris I had a midday talk followed by luncheon with De Gaulle. In several days in Rome I saw all the important government and party officials, and the press carried front-page stories of these meetings. So it went in other capitals. The Bay of Pigs was a setback, but proved only temporary. However, relations with Khrushchev did not develop as favorably as President Kennedy had hoped. His meeting with Khrushchev in Vienna in June proved to be disappointing. Only on the future of Laos did the two men come to an understanding. Khrushchev was still pressing for an acceptance of an independent East Germany and threatened to sign a separate peace treaty with East Germany before the end of the year, claiming this would end Allied rights in Berlin. A most serious crisis followed.

After the East Germans built the Berlin Wall, Khrushchev indicated through Italian Foreign Minister Fanfani a more conciliatory attitude. Tensions continued, however, until the Cuban missile crisis of October 1962.

President Kennedy handled the Cuban missile crisis with consummate skill and induced Khrushchev to take the offensive missiles out of Cuba. He was able to go on to an agreement with him on a limited test ban.[7] The signing and ratification of the Limited Nuclear Test Ban Treaty marked a high water point in our relations with the Soviet Union. There were of course unsolved critical problems, particularly in regard to Germany and Southeast Asia. But the change in less than a year from the Cuban missile crisis to the test ban was so striking that I believe President Kennedy began to think seriously of a visit to the Soviet Union early in his second term should he be re-elected. But President Kennedy was assassinated three months later.

Within a year new personalities were to take over in Moscow. Khrushchev was removed from office, Brezhnev took his place as Secretary of the Party and Kosygin as Chairman of the Council of Ministers. I will discuss these developments in my next talk as they lead directly to the present.

[7] See page 90 for test ban and page 201 on the missile crisis.

Q   Do you believe that there is anything America could have done to assist Chiang, particularly in the latter period when we did withdraw our support?

A   I don't think so. I went to Chunking to talk with Chiang Kai-shek in January 1946. General Marshall was there at the time. Chiang had grave doubts about coming to an agreement for a coalition with the Communists, and he may have been justified in his fears. I asked him why he did not strengthen his government at once by bringing in the Democratic League, which included the leading Chinese intellectuals. They had recently participated in a Consultative Conference which had attempted to reconcile the contending parties. I also asked him why he didn't get rid of some of his warlords and some of the obviously corrupt people around him. He replied that they were the only ones he could count on for support if he brought the Communists into the government.

Perhaps the outcome might have been better if we had had quite a different approach. Looking at things from Moscow, my idea at the time was that we might better accept temporarily a divided China. If we could have prevented Chiang from sending his best troops into Manchuria where they were chewed up, he would have been far better off. It was hopeless for him to expect to take over the rule of Manchuria when he was having difficulty in controlling even the area where his forces were concentrated—southern China.

I also had grave doubts about the attempts to form a coalition government with the Communists. It seemed to me at the time that Chiang was too weak and the Communists too strong for him to have had much of a chance of survival.

In any event, General Marshall was sent out to attempt to mediate between the Nationalists and the Communists, and he did everything he could under his instructions. Despite General Marshall's patience and skill, the reluctance and suspicion of both sides and the inherent weakness of the Kuomintang made successful mediation impossible.

Q   Mr. Harriman, do you think there is anything that the United States could reasonably have done to have prevented the suppression of the Dubcek government in Czechoslovakia by the Soviets in 1968?

A   I can simply say, "No." There is nothing that we could have done. But we will discuss that later when dealing with current matters.

Q   Sulzberger's book *The Long Row of Candles,* suggests that a war was imminent in 1950–51. Many people believed it was. Did you?

A   Was war imminent in 1950–51? Well, we had the war in Korea at that time. That was the only war in which we were involved. If Stalin had been more aggressive in Germany than he was, the Berlin blockade might have led to war in Europe. But I don't think war was imminent at that time, other than the Korean War. Many Europeans were concerned that Stalin might use military force in Europe, and this fear contributed to the decision to establish a unified military force and command structure for NATO.

Of course, if we had crossed the 38th Parallel a second time to reconquer North Korea and bombed mainland China as well, as General MacArthur wanted to do, there would have been a bigger war. But President Truman very wisely said no to that.

Q   What do you think was the reason that Khrushchev
     agreed to give Austria its independence in 1955?

A   Of course I was not privy to his counsel, but he talked
     to me about it later. He said that it was wise to do this,
     but that Molotov had been against it. During the war I
     had found Molotov much more rigid and more difficult
     to deal with even than Stalin, so I could well understand
     this. When talking about the Trieste settlement, Khru-
     shchev told me that Molotov was "more Yugoslav than
     Tito." It is fairly obvious that Molotov did not want to
     give up anything.

     I don't know why Khrushchev wanted to do this. Some
     people thought it was an indication of his willingness to
     give in on East Germany and permit a unified Germany.
     I am sure that wasn't true, because the Kremlin policy is
     never to give up willingly a square inch of territory that's
     been hallowed by Communist rule. Austria had not
     been communized; it had an independent government.

     The Soviets knew they were not doing very well in
     their occupational zone, and I think they felt that a neu-
     tralized Austria would be more satisfactory for them
     than the existing situation, which was causing a good
     deal of friction. You know, a neutral Austria did make
     it more difficult for NATO to operate, as it cut the direct
     North-South communication lines between the Allies.
     This he may have had in mind.

     Rapacki, the Polish Foreign Minister, did propose a
     denuclearized Central Europe, including Germany, sev-
     eral years later, but that was not considered a feasible
     suggestion by the Allies at the time. Khrushchev may
     have wanted to try out the neutralizing of Central Europe,
     including Germany. I think the Soviets have always wanted
     to have as much of a defensive "cushion" around their

territory as possible. They don't want to have unfriendly neighbors as they have with China, and this might have been viewed as a further "cushion" which gave them some more protection. Even in spite of their prowess in nuclear missiles, I feel that when the Russians think about war they still think in terms of armies moving across frontiers.

All of this is, of course, highly speculative.

Q   Mr. Ambassador, would you comment on the motivation of Soviet foreign policy? Do you think the motivation is primarily that of power politics and national power concerns, or of Communist ideology, or are they both equally determining factors?

A   It is a combination of both. Stalin had both. He was a Russian imperialist with ambitions similar to the Czars. He was also utterly determined to promote world Communist revolution with the oracle in Moscow. Since Stalin's death the world situation has changed, but the Kremlin still has both motivations. I will deal with that later.

Q   If you could relive history, what changes would you make in the United States foreign policy during the wartime conferences and what effect that might have had on the future?

A   Well, I don't think much would have been different. You can argue about a lot of different things. People blame Eisenhower for not going to Berlin, but there had been a decision made in which the occupational zones of Germany were set. It was considered important that we should not meet and clash with the Russians, that we should decide in advance the zones each would occupy to avoid that possibility. The agreed zones were considered to be very favorable by our chiefs of staff at the time they were decided upon. They thought the Russians would be much further into Germany than they got and

that we would not have gotten as far as we did. It didn't
work out that way. I am not critical of them for this, as
no one could have foreseen the military events.

Now if we had tried to do what Churchill proposed
after V-E Day—stand on the Elbe until there was a
political settlement about Eastern Europe—I don't think
it would have done any good, and we would then have
been held responsible for the cold war. Furthermore, our
military plans required a redeployment of our forces
in Europe to the Pacific. Churchill wanted to force a
political settlement about the areas occupied by the Red
Army before we withdrew from the Elbe. But even if we
had gotten an agreement and free elections had been
held, the governments elected would, in all probability,
not have lasted. There was, in fact, a free election in
Hungary in 1945 in which the Smallholders party (the
small peasants' party) got over 50 per cent of the votes
and the Communists only about 18 per cent. The government established after this election lasted only a short
time, and the Communists—supported by the Red Army
—took over and squeezed out the others.

There was no way we could have prevented any of
these events in Eastern Europe without going to war with
the Russians. There were a few military people who considered that. This wasn't De Gaulle, but a few French and
American officers talked about going in and cleaning them
up while we had such superiority in air power. It is
perfectly absurd to think the American people would
have stood for it, even if the President wanted to do it,
which he didn't.

I think it was very important that Roosevelt and
Churchill made the effort to come to an agreement with
Stalin. One achievement was the establishment of the

United Nations. With all the disappointments, it has been effective in many activities during the twenty-five years of its life, although handicapped by the differences that exist between the great powers. The fact that Stalin broke the agreements about Eastern Europe exposed his perfidy and aggressive designs. This aroused the suspicion of the West and eventually led to steps for mutual defense.

There is a group of historians who are now attempting to rewrite the history of that time. Arthur M. Schlesinger, Jr., has pointed out that such attempts to rewrite history have happened frequently in the past.[8] These revisionists are creating myths about what happened and what our objectives were. Some of them take facts out of context and try to build up a case for imagined objectives. Some conveniently overlook Stalin's failure to cooperate, his violation of specific agreements and aggressive actions. Of course, I am not talking about those thoughtful analysts who, with the advantage of hindsight, point out more clearly the significance of events and perhaps mistakes than was possible at the time.

The military alternatives were perhaps more obvious than the political. At the time some people wanted us to go to Vienna, up the Ljubljana Gap, and get there before the Russians, instead of landing in the south of France as we did. Yet as things have turned out, Austria is free today anyway.

Churchill was always very much worried about attempting to cross the Channel. It turned out successfully. It would have been disastrous for the British if it hadn't. Churchill wanted to go at Hitler from the south— "the soft underbelly," as he called it. He didn't want to take the risk of crossing the Channel. Stalin, after

8 "Origins of the Cold War," *Foreign Affairs* (October 1967).

having berated and even insulted us for two years for not establishing a second front in Europe by crossing the Channel, said to me after we had successfully landed, "The history of war has never witnessed such a grandiose operation." He added neither Napoleon nor Hitler had dared attempt it. Later, after he had received detailed reports, he spoke to me again about crossing the Channel, as "an unheard of achievement in the history of warfare." The number of men and the vast amount of equipment which had been thrown into France impressed him greatly. He added "the world had never seen an individual operation of such magnitude—an unbelievable accomplishment." He was unconcerned by the fact that he had previously minimized its difficulties and had accused us of cowardice in not having undertaken it before.

Undoubtedly mistakes were made, and undoubtedly many things might have been improved. Your question is an interesting one, and I have thought a lot about it. But the facts are that, although militarily unprepared, we fought a war successfully on two fronts. With our allies in Europe, we completely defeated Hitler, and almost alone we defeated Japan in the Pacific. That was an extraordinary achievement—and particularly as it was done in less than four years. As far as our relations with the Soviet Union since the end of the war are concerned, I doubt whether any different wartime military or political decisions would have had much effect.

One of President Roosevelt's wartime policies that I questioned at the time was his call for unconditional surrender of the Germans. He wanted to be sure not to make the mistake of Wilson's Fourteen Points. However, his attitude was not fully understood. When he announced the policy of unconditional surrender, he stated that he had in mind the case of the Civil War, when General Grant insisted on the unconditional surrender of a Confederate opponent. After he received the surrender, however, General Grant said that the Confederate officers could keep their small arms, and since they would be plowing when they got home, they could take their horses. Roosevelt had in mind a reasonable attitude toward the Germans after Hitler had surrendered. Unfortunately, this attitude never came through, and it may have led the German army to keep on fighting up to the last.

President Roosevelt announced the unconditional surrender policy at a joint press conference with Prime Minister Churchill, at Casablanca in January 1943, and qualified it by the Civil War story. I had dinner that evening with Churchill, and he told me he was greatly upset that the President had announced such an important matter without prior consultation. He felt the policy was a mistake. There had been some consultation and agreement reached between the British and American Chiefs of Staff on this subject, but Churchill maintained that the President should have discussed this subject fully from a political standpoint with him before an announcement of policy was made.

I personally shared Churchill's concern, as I believed the Germans would be more ready to surrender to us than to the Russians, provided they felt our treatment of them would not be too harsh. I raised the subject with the President and recommended that his reasonable attitude toward the German people be repeated and made clearer, but he was adamant. The subject came up in one of my talks with Stalin and he indicated some concern, suggesting that it might make the Germans fight harder. However, he was always suspicious of what we might do, and he readily agreed to the understanding that no one ally would accept the surrender of any enemy unilaterally.

Our Chiefs of Staff were always concerned that Stalin might make a deal with Hitler behind our backs. I never shared this concern, as I was convinced that after the break and the bitter fighting there was no basis for a reconciliation between Stalin and Hitler. As it later developed in connection with the discussion on the possible surrender of the Germans in Italy, Stalin himself was gravely concerned that we might make a separate deal with the Germans. He must have been fully aware of the fact that the Germans were less afraid of the Western Allies than they were of the Russians and that, if Hitler were overthrown, the Germans would be ready to come to most any agreement with the West in order to limit the Red Army advance into their country.

One decision at Potsdam I seriously questioned at the time was the postponement until the peace conference of the definite settlement of the border between Poland and Germany. I felt this would create real friction and difficulty. I strongly supported the State Department's recommendation that the Oder-*Upper* Neisse be agreed to as the western border of Poland. This would have left most of Upper Silesia to Germany with a population of six million, almost all Germans, and avoided the transfer of that many more people.

Stalin argued for the shorter and more westerly Oder-Neisse Line for strategic reasons as being easier to defend. This was a time, I thought, for us to say "no." The humane reason for not uprooting that many more people seemed to me to far outweigh this rather tenuous military argument. In any event, I felt leaving it open was the worst action as it would create tensions in the future. Above all, I felt the border should have been agreed on at the time, and I would have preferred even our acceptance of Stalin's demand to indecision. At the time I felt Jimmie Byrnes made a mistake to propose the compromise which gave Poland administrative responsibility in theory only until the peace conference but practically full possession unless forced out by military action.

This question has caused tensions in the intervening years, and yet now due to Willy Brandt's initiative supported by the statesmanship of the majority of the German people, the question seems to have been peacefully settled. It may have given Willy Brandt some trading cards on his negotiations with the Soviets.

Furthermore, if we had stood firm, Stalin might have agreed to leave Upper Silesia to Germany. That would have been a loss to Poland and strengthened East Germany. Most of the dislocated Germans, I believe, resettled in West Germany and are perhaps happier and more prosperous today.

At the moment, on balance, it appears that the indecisive action taken at Potsdam may have been for the best. This is an example of the impossibility of looking into the future with any certainty.

PRESENT:
Russia/Vietnam

Russia

IN DISCUSSING OUR SUBJECT, THE UNIted States and the Soviet Union in a changing world, we have talked about the past. Now, we will consider the present, including Vietnam, which I know is uppermost in most people's minds. I will, therefore, discuss it in some detail. But Vietnam must be put in perspective as far as the Soviet Union is concerned, and it is important to realize that it is only one of the significant international issues we face today.

In dealing with the Soviet Union, we must recognize that we cannot now have an over-all detente. Their objectives and ours are still at variance. In 1945 I was criticized because I said that Stalin's objectives and our own were irreconcilable and that we had to find a way to compose our differences in order to live together in peace on this small planet.

I still feel the same way about it. But there have been changes of remarkable importance. The Soviet Union has substantially changed, and to a considerable extent we have changed—some for the better, some for the worse. Much of what we have done we have every right to be proud of, yet we are now involved in Vietnam in a manner which is hard to justify.

But first I want to talk a bit about the present leaders in the Soviet Union. We have discussed the change from Stalin to Khrushchev. That was followed in 1964 by the rather sudden replacing of Khrushchev by the present group, of whom the principal personalities are Brezhnev, the Secretary of the Communist Party, and Kosygin, the head of the government, with Podgorny the titular Chief of State in a supporting rule.

When I had the long day and night talk with Khrushchev in 1959, I asked him if Stalin had picked his successor. Khrushchev responded, "Stalin thought he was going to live forever." He explained that this had created serious difficulties when Stalin died and stated, "I am not going to make the same mistake." He turned to Mikoyan, whom he often used as the fall guy for his jokes, and said, "This is one thing Anastas and I agreed on." Then, pointing to Frol Koslov, he said they had agreed on him.

Shortly afterward, Khrushchev announced this to the press. But later Koslov got sick—had a heart attack, so when I had a chance to talk to Khrushchev privately at the time of the Test Ban negotiations in July 1963, I asked him whether he could tell me who was now designated as his successor. He said, "It's true that Koslov has been ill and may not be able to undertake this work, but it has not been decided. Brezhnev is the front-runner, but Podgorny is catching up fast and may overtake him."

Khrushchev told me he was going to retire at seventy. His seventieth birthday was the following April, but curiously enough, he stayed on, and then got the heave-ho in September. Why he did not retire I don't know, because I have not talked to him since, and no outsider has been allowed to talk to him about it. He is in comfortable retirement, but like most everything else in the Soviet Union, he is kept apart from contact with the outside world.

I don't know what happened that caused his fall but I recall one amusing story. Someone associated with the White House asked the CIA why they had failed to inform the President of the imminence of this important change in Soviet leadership. The CIA answered: "If we had known about it, Khrushchev would have known about it, and then it wouldn't have happened."

The CIA gets blamed for most everything. As a matter of fact they keep the government well informed on essential matters. Their solid information frequently acts to prevent the advice of those who see ghosts from being taken seriously.

Some people have suggested that Khrushchev was thrown out because of his bungling attempt to put offensive nuclear missiles in Cuba and then being forced to withdraw them. I have found that Westerners often credit foreign affairs as the reason for Soviet decisions, whereas in my experience with the Soviet Union, I have found in most cases actions were taken because of domestic considerations. In the Politburo, the problems within the Soviet Union of controlling some two hundred million people and every aspect of their lives usually loom far larger than international issues.

For my part, I believe that Khrushchev was ousted largely because of the manner in which he handled domestic affairs. He made snap decisions without full consultation and no doubt built up enmities. He made glaring mistakes in judgment. Perhaps the most obvious related to his encouraging collective farmers to grow corn. He was much influenced by Roswell Garst, an Iowa farmer who came to Moscow and sold him on the importance of hybrid corn.

With his usual enthusiasm, Khrushchev accepted this advice but went too far. He ordered the collective farmers to grow corn as far north as Moscow where the climate was far too cold to permit corn to mature. Enthusiasts in the American Embassy had for years been trying to grow corn in the Embassy garden. Once they triumphantly succeeded in producing ears three inches long! The damage to Soviet agriculture in such a widespread attempt must have been extremely costly.

He ordered vast areas of virgin land plowed for wheat. As I saw for myself in 1959, some of these areas were extremely carefully cultivated, based on American and particularly Canadian experience in the "dust bowls." However, others were undoubtedly carelessly handled, contributing to the great dust storm of 1963.

In addition, Khrushchev's attempt to reorganize the Party and the government into separate rural and urban hierarchies turned many members of the Central Committee against him.

Whatever the details of the criticisms, I am satisfied that Khrushchev was "retired" because his colleagues felt that he made too many impetuous decisions, without full consultation.

In speaking of a successor, it is interesting that Khrushchev didn't mention Kosygin's name. That is because Kosygin was involved more as a *government* than a *Party* official, and to the Communists the Secretary of the Party is the job that counts the most. The Party has the last word in the battles between the government administrators and the Party.

It isn't clear just what the division of authority is among the present leaders and how they are working together. Obviously Brezhnev as Secretary of the Party holds the key job and appears to be gaining authority. But there evidently is agreement against the "cult of personality"—one man glorified and in full control. This is partly because they fear a return of the arbitrary ruthlessness that existed under Stalin which could be turned on them. Also, they don't want a repetition of what they regarded as Khrushchev's erratic policies and failure to consult his colleagues. Since the Kremlin leaders themselves are no longer willing to risk the uncertainty of Stalinist capricious purges, the people as a whole are free from the terror of one-man arbitrary rule.

But let me quickly say that controls are still very rigid. They are not as indiscriminate as they used to be and not quite as arbitrary. There are some sort of hearings or court action, and people know what has happened to the accused. However, there is in no sense what we would consider anywhere near adequate protection for the defendant.

Kosygin is the head of the government. He has been in administration a long time. As a young man he was a worker in a textile factory and rose to factory manager. I met him first with Mikoyan in 1942, when he was involved in light industry production. He was then particularly anxious to get from the United States under Lend-Lease raw materials for production of things the Red Army needed—wool for blankets and uniforms, hide for boots, and so forth. I talked to him about these things during the war. I saw him again in '59 when he was head of the Gosplan, the central economic planning agency for the entire Soviet Union. Then later, in 1965, when he was Chairman of the Council of Ministers, I had several long talks with him. Of course, I met him again at Glassboro with President Johnson in 1967.

He has been a member of the Party throughout that period. He was a member of the Central Committee from 1939 on, and has been on and off the Politburo since 1948. He has long been in the inner councils of the Party. I feel he is ready to fight vigorously for what he thinks best, but when the Party decides, he accepts the decisions. He is independent in his own thinking—within the limits of the system.

Kosygin is most serious and sober in discussions—entirely devoid of Khrushchev's interjections of humor, boisterousness or threats. Although he does not threaten in the way Khrushchev did, he states emphatically the dangers that he sees developing from our differences. In my talks with him, I always felt I knew where we stood with him. He is tough-minded, but at the same time he tries to understand our point of view. I believe that he wants to come to understandings with us in as wide a field as possible and that in the Kremlin councils he takes the more reasonable position as opposed to the hard-liners.

I don't know Brezhnev, and so my understanding of him comes largely secondhand and from talking to people who knew him. For instance, Tito told me the last time I saw him, in 1967, that he knew Brezhnev well and found him reasonable, but commented that he had not had as much experience with Kosygin as I had. In answer to my question he said that he did not believe Brezhnev was dominated by the military. Tito evidently had no inkling of the hard-line he later developed in the invasion of Czechoslovakia and the Brezhnev Doctrine.

As Secretary of the Party, it is within Brezhnev's responsibility to maintain Party ideology and Party discipline. In the present crackdown on the intellectuals and freedom of expression, Brezhnev must be directly involved.

My impression is that Kosygin is not as hard-line, but he is a devout Communist—a disciple of the Faith. I felt that Stalin thought of himself as the prophet. He thought that in time Communist ideology would be known as Marxism-Leninism-Stalinism, and if he were alive today he would be quite disappointed he did not achieve that position. He wasn't a disciple. He interpreted Marxism-Leninism as he saw fit.

Kosygin is a disciple. He still believes that Communism is going to sweep the world. He still believes that the few—the Communist Party—should decide for the many how man is destined to live. Naturally, I am totally convinced that the main thrust of human effort is toward the freedom and dignity of the individual, governments responsive to the will of the people, and all the basic freedoms we value so greatly.

I talked with Kosygin about Castro. My guess is that the

Soviets are a little bored with him. He plays up to Peking too much. He is an expensive luxury, but they can't afford to let him down. He is the symbol of Communism in the Western Hemisphere.

I am inclined to believe that the main Soviet policy in Latin America is to support, as in Chile, the legalized Communist parties in their attempts to form popular fronts with other leftist parties.[1] In this manner they hope to gain a position in the government through constitutional procedures. Of course, the eventual Communist objective is to get control by squeezing out the other parties and by suppressing democratic constitutional procedures. It will be of intense interest to watch developments in Chile.

However, the Soviets are also supporting the Cuban efforts to activate insurgencies in Latin America. Russian instructors have been in Cuba to train young Latin Americans brought there from different countries in subversion and guerrilla warfare. Russian equipment is made available.

I asked Kosygin why the Soviets were doing this; why they were training these young men to create trouble. I referred to Venezuela as an example. I pointed out it was one of the most democratic countries in Latin America. Elections had been held, and the government was attempting to make social progress—perhaps not as fast as some people want, but it was moving in the right direction. I asked him why should these few guerrillas be sent in to disrupt this effort.

He said, "But they speak for the people."

"But they don't," I replied. "They couldn't. There is just a handful of them."

Again he reiterated that they speak for the people. I then realized that in speaking about this handful, Kosygin had in mind the few Bolsheviks that arrived at Petrograd in March

[1] Statement made prior to the Chilean election of September 1970.

1917, took leadership of the party, and within a year gained control of the government. They claimed to speak for the people then, and their successors still do so today.

So that is Kosygin's conception. And as long as the Soviet leaders are ready to support the use of force to impose their will and their doctrine on other people, we are going to have trouble; we are going to have clashes; we are going to have confrontations.

However, I think Kosygin personally is more interested in meeting the goals of economic development within the Soviet Union. The Soviets have done great things in expanding heavy industry but only a mediocre job in meeting the consumer needs of their people. Kosygin recognizes that, if Communism is to be accepted in the world, they have to show more progress in improved standards of living for the people than they have after half a century of rule in Russia. This is all to the good. Kosygin is less willing to take risks than Stalin nor to put the energy and resources into foreign adventures at the expense of internal needs. I think he would like to see conditions develop that would permit a sharp reduction in the cost of supporting Hanoi or Cairo. That's my guess about him. But his is not the only voice.

Yet there is generally a tendency toward more concern about meeting the material needs of the Russian people, and this results in a greater willingness to come to understandings with us. I believe a real opportunity exists to negotiate settlements on specific issues where our interests coincide or can be reconciled. Despite some of the rhetoric of the Nixon Administration, the "era of negotiations" did not begin in 1969. We have been able to negotiate agreements from time to time, but I think the opportunities are greater now than they have been, provided we take advantage of them.

A Washington *Post* editorial of February 19, 1969, pointed

out that President Kennedy started the move from confrontation to negotiation. But even President Kennedy was not the first President to negotiate successful agreements with the Soviets.

Some people seem to think that we should not try to come to agreements with the Soviets because they don't keep them. However, a number of agreements that have been reached have worked out well, for example the Austrian State Treaty and the limited test ban. Such agreements, which are either self-enforcing or can be monitored unilaterally, can be very much in our own interest. And each agreement helps reduce mutual suspicions, and that encourages progress toward understandings on other, perhaps more difficult, issues.

One of the places where we can make progress today is in Europe. The German government is now led by Willy Brandt. He wants to break down the barriers between East and West by the movement of people, thoughts, and goods. He has reversed Adenauer's policy of the Hallstein Doctrine under which West Germany refused to have diplomatic relations with countries that had recognized East Germany. He is meeting with the East German Premier and engaging in serious political and economic negotiations with the Soviets,[2] Poles, and Romanians.

This is a significant movement forward. It is very much to our interest, and I have believed in it for a dozen or more years.

As a matter of fact, I talked to Adenauer about it in 1959. I was then a private citizen. He was quite annoyed with me, because I urged him to accept East Germany's existence on a *de*

---

[2] In August 1970 Kosygin and Brandt signed a Soviet-West German treaty which is subject to ratification after progress has been made on Berlin issues.

facto basis, taking a similar approach to the one Willy Brandt is now.

I had had a good talk with the German Ambassador while I was in Moscow, and Adenauer's statements did not jibe with the Ambassador's judgment. Adenauer was, I gathered, getting information from a source outside of his Embassy that seemed to me to be inaccurate. He underestimated the technological advance the Russians had made since the war and the changes within the Kremlin. I had enormous respect for Chancellor Adenauer and didn't want to pursue the subject further, so I turned to some more agreeable subjects. When it came time for lunch he took me into the dining room where his other guests had assembled. By way of introduction he announced, "Governor Harriman and I have agreed on one thing—it's time for lunch."

I don't think the Nixon Administration has been as enthusiastic in support of Willy Brandt as it might be. When asked whether we would encourage NATO to join in a European security conference between NATO and Warsaw Pact countries, a State Department official took a go-slow attitude. He indicated we would have to review everything. Why don't we get these discussions started? Of prime importance is consideration of a mutual, balanced reduction of force levels. This is the soundest way to reduce the number of American troops in Europe.

Reluctance to move ahead is my fundamental objection to the Administration's attitude in other fields. Take East-West trade as an example. In the President's Message to Congress he says: "We look forward to the time when our relations with communist countries will have improved to the point where trade relations can increase between us."

This suggests that the Soviets must pay some political

concessions for the right to buy from us. This approach is not merely fruitless but harmful. The Soviets can buy practically everything they need from Western Europe and Japan. Trade between these countries and Eastern Europe is now over ten billion dollars a year in each direction, whereas ours is of insignificant volume. This trade is in non-strategic goods; a committee of the OECD in Paris, in which we participate, agrees to a list of strategic items which are not to be sold.

Expanded East-West trade in non-strategic goods could be commercially profitable as well as a step toward better relations. Today it has wider support in the business community than ever before. If the Administration took strong leadership, I believe the Congress would act to remove legislative restrictions. Aside from losing business, our failure to trade normally with the Soviet Union strengthens the influence of the hard-liners in Moscow. In my talks with Mr. Khrushchev, Mr. Kosygin, and other Russians, they have consistently indicated that they consider our trade restrictions as an indication that we have little desire to develop better relations. It is a needless affront.

The adverse effect of our unwillingness to trade with the Soviet Union as other Western countries do is psychological. The economic impact is relatively insignificant. To the Russians it is an indication of unfriendliness toward them. The question of trade came up in my talks with Mr. Khrushchev at the time of the test ban negotiations in July 1963. He said: "We don't care whether the United States sells us anything; what we want is that the United States abolish its discriminatory laws or else there can be no confidence." He added: "Trade is the first sign of neighborly relations. He who did not want to trade, wanted war." As always, Khrushchev stated his ideas rather bluntly—even crudely. But he expressed Russian reactions in an earthy way.

We have even restricted economic relations with Tito. He defied Stalin and has since refused to be dominated by Moscow. Although his is a Communist country, he considers himself non-aligned in his foreign policy. He criticized Moscow for invading Czechoslovakia and rejected the Brezhnev Doctrine. However, the Yugoslavs trade with Cuba, and because of this, congressional inhibitions restrict our economic relations with them. Tito and the Yugoslavs are proud people. They are not going to let our Congress tell them who they should trade with any more than they let Moscow dictate their policy. It is high time that people understand that sovereign countries resent our attempts to dictate policy to them. Such attempts are counter-productive.

For the long range, the most vital negotiations being held today are SALT (the Strategic Arms Limitation Talks). It is a moment in history when both sides find it to their interest to end this disastrous arms race. Restraint in the arms race not only would save vast wasteful expenditures, but understandings in the field will tend to reduce the awesome danger of a nuclear war.

When I talked to Mr. Kosygin in 1965, he said it was going to be very difficult to make progress in this field as long as we were attacking what he called "a sister Socialist state," namely North Vietnam. Fortunately we have been able to make considerable progress in spite of our differences over Vietnam. We have made significant agreements, including treaties on excluding nuclear weapons from outer space and the ocean bed, and on non-proliferation.

When Mr. Kosygin was in the United States in 1967, President Johnson and Secretary McNamara attempted to get negotiations started for the limitation of nuclear weapons. We were insisting that both defensive ABMs, as well as offensive weapons, be considered at the same time. No agreement was reached then, but I felt that Mr. Kosygin's visit to the United States was helpful if for no other reason than that he got a sense of the attitude of the American people. The small college town of Glassboro, where the meetings took place, was filled with people anxious to see him and in spite of the rain they waited for him to appear. When he did appear with President Johnson, he was warmly greeted with resounding applause, and his brief remarks were well received. I could see that he was deeply moved, and I think the experience did a lot of good. Unfortunately, few of the Soviet leaders have had a chance to come to the United States. In fact, they haven't traveled much abroad outside the Soviet orbit.

Apart from the reluctance to proceed with SALT because of Vietnam, the Soviets also seemed at that time to have felt that closer balance between their nuclear forces and ours had to exist before they could consider comprehensive nuclear restraints. In the summer of 1968 the Russians finally agreed to undertake negotiations with us for nuclear restraint. President Johnson took the discussions so seriously that he wanted them to be kicked off with a personal meeting between Chairman Kosygin and himself. Unhappily, the very morning that our allies were to have been notified that a meeting between the two men would take place, the Soviets invaded Czechoslovakia. In the atmosphere of tension that resulted, obviously no meeting could be held.

President Johnson kept President-elect Nixon informed in detail of the earlier discussions and even indicated that negotiations might be started prior to Nixon's inauguration under conditions and circumstances to which the new President might agree. This was not done, and regrettably, it took the new Administration months before offering a date for negotiations. Finally a date five months after President Nixon's inauguration was proposed. This delay probably caused some suspicion in Moscow. In the meantime, both sides went ahead with development and testing. The Soviets continued their increased deployment of inter-continental ballistic missiles (ICBMs), including their giant SS-9s and testing of their multiple war heads, and we went ahead with our program for anti-ballistic missiles (ABMs) and multiple independently targeted re-entry vehicles (MIRVs).

Substantive talks did not in fact begin until April 1970, although preliminary talks took place in November 1969. During this period of nearly two years, both sides made substantial developments. On our side, we were moving ahead rapidly in the development of MIRVs and deployment of ABMs, and the Soviets were moving ahead as well. A number of people had urged President Nixon a year earlier to follow the example of President Kennedy and announce that our testing and deployment would be held up if the other side took similar restraints. For some reason, this was not done.

Instead, there were a number of provocative statements from the Pentagon. Among them was the assertion that we must have nuclear "superiority." That was fortunately superseded by acceptance of the idea of "sufficiency," though without defining the meaning. It was also said that an agreement would benefit the Russians more than us; that we could afford the nuclear arms race and they couldn't. Then came accusations that, according to secret information, the Kremlin was planning a first strike, although this was later denied by the Secretary of State. Finally, shortly before substantive negotiations began in

Vienna, the first deployment of MIRV war heads was announced to take place in two months. All this may have contributed to Soviet delays in beginning the talks and confused the situation.

I believe that an agreement can be reached, but I am fearful that the delays have been costly and that the agreement may not be as comprehensive nor the ceiling on nuclear weapons as low as it might have been had the discussions taken place earlier and in a more favorable atmosphere with mutual postponement of developments.

Negotiations for the nuclear test ban in 1963 were commenced in most propitious circumstances, as President Kennedy had announced that he would stop testing as long as the other side did the same. This was an indication to Khrushchev that Kennedy was serious.

There were, of course, a few advisers to the President, as now, who were opposed to any practical agreement. A few scientists and certain of the military believed that our security can best be protected by continuing the arms race regardless of cost and counting on our ability to keep ahead. The overwhelming majority of scientists strongly believe that our interests are best protected if agreements for mutual restraint can be reached with the Soviet Union. They testified in support of Senate ratification of the limited test ban treaty. A few testified against the treaty, pointing to barely conceivable possibilities. At the time it was even suggested that the Soviets could carry on clandestine testing behind the moon! After full hearing and debate, the test ban treaty was approved—eighty to nineteen.

The most important factor in the success of the test ban negotiations was that President Kennedy seized the initiative by stating in June at American University:

To make clear our good faith and solemn con-
victions on the matter, I now declare that the United
States does not propose to conduct nuclear tests in
the atmosphere as long as other states do not do so.
We will not be the first to resume. Such a declaration
is no substitute for a formal binding treaty—but I
hope it will help us achieve one.

That was a signal to Khrushchev, and he responded encour-
agingly about the test ban in an otherwise rather intransigent
speech in East Germany the first week in July.

President Kennedy and Prime Minister Macmillan had agreed
that the negotiations should be moved from Geneva to Moscow and should be conducted on a higher level. It was hoped
that this would break the tedious impasse in Geneva and that
with a fresh start and a fresh team there would be a better
chance for an agreement. Khrushchev fell in line with this approach.

Macmillan appointed Lord Hailsham, Lord President of the
Council and Minister of Science, and President Kennedy selected me. I was particularly encouraged by the fact that we
were going to meet in Moscow, as this meant that we would
have direct contact with Chairman Khrushchev, the man of
final authority. Of course, I knew Foreign Minister Gromyko
would handle the details of the negotiations, but he would be
able to consult constantly with Khrushchev. And this is the way
it worked out.

I was extremely fortunate in the team that was selected to go
with me. To be successful in negotiations, it is important that a
team possess certain characteristics. Obviously, the members
must be capable, well-informed men. Equally important is that
the judgment of each individual should carry weight in Washington with the department or agency with which he is associ-

ated. And our team certainly did. Carl Kaysen of the White House staff was highly regarded by the President and Mac Bundy as well. John McNaughton was General Counsel of the Defense Department, and his judgment was highly respected by Secretary of Defense McNamara. Adrian Fisher, deputy director of the Arms Control and Disarmament Agency (ACDA), had worked long and intimately with William Foster, the director. William Tyler, Assistant Secretary for Europe, stood well in the State Department. Frank Long had the confidence of the scientists in and out of government.

This well-balanced team was able to deal with the unforeseen difficulties that arose in the negotiations. My colleagues had the imagination, initiative, and knowledge to propose compromises which protected our own interests and yet overcame the Soviet objections. Their recommendations carried weight and led to quick decisions in Washington.

On our arrival in Moscow, one of the questions I was asked by the newspapermen was, "How long is this going to take?" The normal answer, and the one they expected, was that it might take months. I was afraid that might be true, but I replied: "I know that President Kennedy wants an agreement, and I believe that Chairman Khrushchev does. If we will meet each other with sincerity, we can reach an agreement rapidly and we ought to be out of here in two weeks." I guess they thought I was crazy, and I myself felt I was being over-optimistic. But I thought a target date would put pressure on the Soviets, and as it turned out, they did get us out in exactly two weeks. The daily discussions were long and intensive, but what was most surprising was the promptness with which we got counterproposals to reconcile impasses.

Hailsham and I, with a couple of our advisers, had a more than three-hour talk with Khrushchev the afternoon following our arrival. Khrushchev got right down to business and said: "Since we have decided to have a test ban, let us sign now and fill in the details later."

I agreed, and handed him a blank sheet of paper, saying: "Fine, you sign first."

This was typical of my experience with Khrushchev. He was in dead earnest, but often had a light way of saying things— sometimes in order to get your reaction. I interpreted his jocular suggestion at this time to mean that he had made up his mind he wanted an agreement and was going to make every effort to come to terms.

He then underlined the serious importance of nuclear arms control. He said people were awaiting results of these meetings not only because of concern for the burden of military expenditures but for life itself. He said: "The accumulation of armaments has throughout history led to war and destruction of human beings, including those who accumulated the arms." He added: "Today both the robbers and those robbed are in equal positions, since both will be annihilated in nuclear war."

After speaking soberly about the importance of our coming to an agreement, he turned to a lighter vein. He said he was glad to see me again but took me to task for not having undertaken the job he had offered me in 1959 as his economic adviser. He had jokingly proposed this when I was asking him questions about how he was going to overcome certain of his economic difficulties.

He then returned to serious discussion, saying: "In order to save time, I want to tell you right away that the Soviet government will not agree to any [on-site] inspection—not even the two or three we had proposed before. But we will agree to the black boxes." (These were locked and tamper-proof seismographic sensors to be positioned in a number of places in each country.) He claimed that on-site inspection was "outmoded" and that there was no point in arguing about it. If we did not agree to a comprehensive test ban without inspection, he was ready to come to an agreement on a limited three-environments ban, namely in the atmosphere, under water, and in outer space. Underground was excluded.

When Hailsham and I tried to get him to permit our scientists to consult with his scientists on ways to differentiate between underground nuclear explosions and natural earthquakes, he would have none of it. He said again there was no use talking about on-site inspection, as this was disguised espionage. When I tried to assure him that we had no such objective in mind, Khrushchev replied: "You remind me of a cat saying that he would only eat mice and not the bacon lying in the room." He added that he would not trust such a cat, "as it would undoubtedly snatch the bacon when no one was in the room."

Khrushchev said further: "There is no need for discussions among the scientists, since we are now talking about a three-environments ban." Hailsham tried to argue with Khrushchev about inspection, but Khrushchev brushed him aside and said: "I know what cats are like."

After some further discussions which were very much to the point, Khrushchev gave us a Soviet draft of a three-environments ban treaty, and Hailsham and I gave him our draft. It was agreed that we would meet with Gromyko the next day to reconcile the differences. Khrushchev suggested that if there were matters that could not be resolved with Gromyko, he himself was prepared to discuss them with us. As it turned out, we were able to reach agreement with Gromyko, but there is no doubt that Gromyko was in touch with Khrushchev between our meetings, and when an impasse was reached involving the Soviet position, the next day he came back with a compromise position. Gromyko himself did not have the authority to agree to compromises. Of course neither did we. But we got prompt consideration from Washington of our recommendation—in fact, due to the time difference, overnight replies. I felt this was to no small extent due to President Kennedy's personal interest in obtaining constructive results from the negotiations.

Oddly enough, one of the points with which we had the greatest difficulty from the very beginning was the withdrawal clause. We had proposed that a party to the treaty could withdraw on reasonable notice if atmospheric testing occurred, which in its opinion jeopardized its security. Gromyko took the firm position, among other arguments, that our proposal compromised his government's sovereign right to renounce a treaty when it was no longer in its interest to adhere to it.

I insisted that we honored our treaty commitments and that this treaty must provide for withdrawal only on the basis of specific events in the nuclear field threatening our security. We had in mind, of course, the possibility of developments by Red China which might require renewed testing. In any event, the Senate would not ratify the treaty without a reasonable withdrawal clause. I told Gromyko bluntly that this was a "must" for us. Gromyko still demurred and accused me of demanding one-sided concessions. I stood firm, and for a while it looked as if we had reached an impasse.

Hailsham was much upset. He informed Prime Minister Macmillan that my rigidity was jeopardizing negotiations. Macmillan instructed British Ambassador Harlech to ask President Kennedy to call me off. I learned of this later, as, needless to say, President Kennedy sent me no such instructions.

Gromyko came up with a substitute withdrawal clause including the phrase, "exercising its national sovereignty . . ." and not limiting the reasons for withdrawal. We accepted the phrase, but insisted and later got agreement on language satisfactory to us limiting the reasons for withdrawal to events in the field of the treaty. The withdrawal clause was the type of issue, but not the only one, which could not have been resolved so promptly if we had not been negotiating in Moscow.

I had an opportunity to talk informally with Khrushchev on Sunday, July 21, at the Soviet-American track meet. Khrushchev showed up unexpectedly with Hungarian Prime Minister Kadar, and asked me to join him in his official box. I talked with him about a number of things. At one point, during a lull in competition, he asked me, "How are you getting along with Gromyko?" I replied, "I get about as much out of Gromyko as you can squeeze out of a stone." He asked, "What are your difficulties?" I replied, "Our major difficulty is about withdrawal." He quickly shied away, saying: "I don't want to hear about it—I made a diplomatic blunder—I never should have brought the subject up!" I added, "I hope anyway that you instruct Gromyko to be cooperative."

Perhaps our greatest difficulty was getting Khrushchev to abandon his insistence on a non-aggression pact between the NATO and Warsaw Pact countries, to be agreed to at the same time as the test ban. This subject was impossible for us to deal with as we could not speak for the other NATO countries.

Of course, there were concessions we had to make. We broke some crockery in Washington by eliminating the exception we had proposed permitting atmosphere explosions for "Plowshare" (use of nuclear explosions for peaceful purposes such as excavating canals or harbors). This was one of the subjects we had talked over in Washington before our departure. Jerome Wiesner,[3] Scientific Adviser to the President, had been most helpful in pointing out that the Plowshare

---

[3] Professor at the Massachusetts Institute of Technology.

projects were remote and should not stand in the way of a test ban treaty.

On this point, however, we established a negotiating record which should make it possible for us to take up with the Soviet Union a modification to deal with a Plowshare type of project should it be seriously considered. I talked with Khrushchev himself about this, and he assured me that if nuclear excavation became practicable, we would not find it difficult to come to an understanding. In fact, the Russians themselves are thinking about mountain-moving projects.

Another major difficulty arose in connection with the adherence to the treaty of governments and regimes that one of us did not recognize. Although all three of us wanted the maximum feasible adherence, our widely differing recognition policies toward certain governments and the intense emotion which lay behind them created major obstacles. To overcome them we devised a unique and flexible procedure (I think it originated in Adrian Fisher's fertile mind), and as it turned out, 106 governments have signed the treaty. The treaty could be signed in all of the three capitals or in any one of them, and a government signing in one of the three capitals would be fully bound to the treaty. The procedure took care of our problems, such as East Germany, but it did not satisfy the Russians. Gromyko maintained that there were certain governments they did not recognize but that they knew existed, such as Spain, whereas they would not admit that the Chinese Nationalist government in Taipei even existed.

This took hours to work out. We finally came to an oral understanding that if any one were asked about its attitude toward a signatory it didn't recognize, it was free to express its attitude toward the regime. This was the last remaining subject and came to a head late in the afternoon of July 25. Gromyko seemed keen to initial the agreement that evening, as everything else had been agreed to. For our part, we had to get the President's approval of this unique and complex arrangement. Carl Kaysen undertook to get Mac Bundy on the telephone and attempt to get the President's immediate approval. We placed the call to the White House from Spiridonovka House, where our meetings took place. By fortunate coincidence, Mac Bundy happened to be with the President in the Situation Room, and we were able to get the President's immediate approval to these arrangements, including the oral understanding.

I returned to the conference and said to Gromyko, "Well, where are the copies of the treaty we are to initial?" This took Gromyko by surprise, and I tried to explain that Mr. Kaysen had been a successful operator on the telephone. We found it was impossible to translate the difference between an "operator on the telephone" and a "telephone operator." In this spirit of good humor we proceeded to the gratifying task of initialing the copies of the treaty in both Russian and English. The Russians were struck by the fact that my British colleague, Lord Hailsham, initialed with the single letter "H." It looked a bit like a football goal post.

Khrushchev was delighted, and an incident occurred that showed the difference between Stalin's Russia and Khrushchev's. Stalin kept aloof from the public except for rare unannounced appearances at the Bolshoi. He lived in the Kremlin, and when he went to his dacha from the Kremlin, he traveled at high speed, with a car in front and a car behind. His car had bulletproof glass. Traffic at intersections was held up. The Kremlin was his fortress and no one was allowed in. Khrushchev opened it up. It's a public park today, with women and their children playing in it and floods of visitors to the historic buildings.

The afternoon following the initialing of the test ban treaty, I called on Chairman Khrushchev at his office, and after our conversation he suggested we walk over together to the dinner he was giving our Anglo-American group. It was to be a small group; I was glad it wasn't one of those Stalin state banquets. We walked from his office through the Kremlin to the Great Palace. On the way we ran into quite a large crowd in front of the Palace of Congresses. It is a big modern building right in the middle of the Kremlin, which offends some people. I don't mind it because good architecture even of different styles blends together, and somehow this does.

Khrushchev stopped. He pinched a little girl on the cheek and patted another on the head. Then he said to the crowd, "This is Gaspodin Garriman." That is Mr. Harriman in Russian. "He has just signed a test ban agreement. I am going to take him to dinner. Do you think he deserves his dinner?" He got a cheer. He talked as an American politician would with a crowd.

Now there has been some tightening up, unfortunately, and events in Czechoslovakia have been most discouraging. But I am utterly convinced that there is a trend toward greater freedom, which no one can stop. It's not a straight line up. It's a curve that goes up and back, and we are on the down swing now.

A major event in that hardening was the invasion of Czechoslovakia. I had been very much impressed with the fact that in January 1968 the Czech Communist Party itself decided to permit far greater freedom. It wasn't opponents of the Communist Party, as had been the case in Poland, East Germany, and Hungary. The Communist Party itself adopted a freer policy toward the press and other forms of public expression. The tragedy was that things went somewhat too far too fast to suit the Kremlin and, apparently on a close decision, the Soviets decided to intervene. Ulbricht may have told them, "You will lose East Germany if you permit this." Or the primary reason may have been the Soviet leaders' concern for the effect the Czech example would have on their own internal situation. Perhaps the failure of the Czech government to control press attacks on the Soviet Union, as they had agreed to, was the last straw.

The Soviets tried to rationalize the intervention by the so-called Brezhnev Doctrine.[4] The announcement of this doctrine shocked people the world over and met with vigorous opposition even within the Communist ranks. The governments of Yugoslavia and Romania have rejected it, and important Communist parties such as those in Italy and France have expressed disapproval. I am inclined to believe that even in Communist countries whose leaders accepted it, the doctrine was not popular with the people.

The intervention was a great tragedy, but it isn't the end of the battle. People have been encouraged to stand up— even in the Soviet Union—and there is a difference from the Stalin period.

I will try to give you a picture of what the difference is. For instance, there was the case of Pavel Litvinov, the grandson of Maxim Litvinov, former Foreign Minister and wartime Ambassador here. This young man went into Red Square with a placard opposing the Czech invasion—"Get out of Czechoslovakia." He was picked up, of course. He was tried, sentenced to five years imprisonment, and at least we know where he is. In Stalin's day he would not have gotten

[4] The Brezhnev Doctrine announced the "right" and "duty" of countries of the "Socialist Commonwealth" to intervene in the affairs of one of their number if Communism seemed threatened in that country.

to Red Square. He would have been grabbed before, and his body would never have been seen again. This is a change. It isn't as much of a change as we would like, but it is a beginning.

An ominous development which has come to light in recent years is the shocking procedure of diagnosing as mentally deranged those dissidents and authors whose writings are considered objectionable. This practice was inherited from czarist days and Stalin used it extensively, at times to punish those who left the Party and began going to church. It was condemned by Khrushchev in his exposure of Stalin, but evidently it was not entirely abandoned. Under it people are committed to mental institutions by administrative decision without trial. Zhores Medvedev, the biologist detained under this procedure, was released after strong protest by distinguished Soviet scientists. His release was hailed throughout the world, and we can only hope that the revulsion this case caused will lead in time to the abolition of this appalling practice.

Another interesting thing is the well-developed system of underground publications—*samizdat*—which is something they can't stop. If there is a novel or a poem that doesn't pass muster, it is put on a typewriter and then passed from one hand to another. People who get it help type copies and pass them on. There is a surprisingly big circulation in that way. Therefore things are not as tight as under Stalin. But there is still an attempt to control what is written by strictly controlling what is published. That is why unauthorized publication abroad is considered so serious a crime.

There is one thing which I believe is a fundamental failure in the Soviet Union. The Soviets took over a country which was perhaps 70 to 75 per cent illiterate, one of the backward countries of Europe, and with great cost and effort they changed it into one of the most literate. There is hardly any illiteracy left at all.

But their objective was to create what they called the "New Soviet Man," and I think they have failed in achieving this as fully as they had hoped. The hope was that their education system would equip people with technical skills, but in addition would embue them with a deep belief in Communist dogma and complete acceptance of Party dictates. Under Stalin all methods of communication were controlled. Private discussions even within a family were spied on and reported. There has been an attempt to continue the control of communication, but there is much more freedom of discussion in private, although contact with foreigners is watched and discouraged.

However I have gathered the impression that Soviet students generally, except for a few ardent believers in the Faith, are bored with the indoctrination. They want to read what they would like. They want to discuss and write what they like. Of course, they resent restrictions on such things as listening to Voice of America broadcasts of American popular music. Above all, they want to travel. They resent the fact that they are not allowed to travel.

This is one of the reasons why I am so much opposed to restrictions of Americans to travel. I went to the Soviet Union in 1926, when the United States didn't recognize it. I was told very solemnly that I went at my own risk and that if I got into trouble I was on my own. That's as it should be.

In 1959 I wanted to go to Red China and would have gone if the Chinese authorities had let me in, but they very politely sent me a message that it wasn't convenient that year. It was quite unusual to get any answer. I was planning to go even if I did not get State Department approval. I might have had a legal struggle on my hands that I was ready to take to the Supreme Court.

I consider freedom of travel to be a basic American right, and I resent interference with it except under wartime conditions. I think it is a good thing for those youngsters who want to go to Cuba and work in the cane fields to go at their own risk and get some hard work under their belts. Why shouldn't they go? What are we afraid of? Americans ought to be able to go anywhere they want—but at their own risk if we don't recognize the country.

It is perfectly true that Soviet students are affected by their education and environment. They believe in their economic system. They couldn't care less that the government not the Bethlehem Steel Company produces steel. It doesn't bother them one iota that the government owns the means of production. In fact, they defend it. They are quite satisfied that their economic system is all right—although they share the general desire for more consumer goods and are critical of the inefficiency. Although they accept the regulated routine of Soviet life as normal, they seem to want more flexibility to lead their own lives and to develop their own ideas. That is encouraging, and that is going to continue.

So in my mind there is hope. I decry the "old cold war warriors" who don't understand that things are moving—even though haltingly—and are not willing to support policies which will encourage this. As one example, this business about not trading with the Russians—can you imagine the effect when the young Soviet people realize that we are not willing to trade with their country? It prejudices them against us. It makes it easier for the ideologists and hard-liners to stimulate suspicion and hostility toward us.

At the same time, I don't agree at all with those who think that all we have to do is to love them and everything will be all right. Those who say that the only difference between the United States and the Soviet Union is a difference in economic theory and practice are mistaken. As I explained in regard to Kosygin, their ultimate objectives are very different from ours and they are still as determined as ever. They believe that they have the truth by which all men are destined to live. They believe in the concept of a few taking control and forcing the rest of the people to accept their dictates. I am convinced they are on the wrong track, and we should not be afraid to compete.

In the Middle East, although the Soviets are determined to expand their influence at our expense, I had hoped we could at least find a way to end the war. I am quite disappointed; I had hoped we could make some permanent progress there. I think the Russians were humiliated to see a billion dollars' worth of their best military equipment strewn over the Sinai Desert in the Six-Day War. I also think that they believe that Israel can still outmatch the Arabs. I saw Nasser himself on television say, "It isn't a question of planes, it's a question of pilots. The Israelis have two pilots for every plane. We have only one pilot for every two planes." But it isn't only the number of pilots, it's their quality. If the spirit in Israel continues, I don't think there is going to be an explosion.

I don't think the Soviets want a renewed war. But it is a dangerous situation, intensified by the growing Palestinian Arab intransigence.[5]

There is no doubt that the Soviets want to push our influence out of the Middle East. Stalin himself tried to move into the Mediterranean. At Potsdam, he asked for a base in Libya. He suggested to Churchill that there was an area in North Africa under British control—a desert—and asked that the Soviets be given a base there. Of course, Churchill re-

[5] For further discussion of Middle East see page 183.

fused, pointing out that Libya was not their territory. Truman was firm. He offered instead right of transit in all international waters everywhere in the world, including the Danube and the Rhine. The Soviets were offered right of transit everywhere—even the Panama Canal. However, Stalin balked at the idea of free transit in the Danube, and that ended the discussion.

The Russians have been after increased influence in the Middle East and the Mediterranean for quite a while. The Czars aspired to it. People now are shocked to see the growth of Soviet naval forces, particularly in this area. But this has been planned for a long time. Stalin once told me that no nation could be a world power without a merchant marine and a navy, so I have not been surprised that the Soviets have developed a naval force. Nevertheless, their presence in the Mediterranean does complicate and make the situation more dangerous.

For the present time, the Soviets are making progress with the Arabs. They are supporting the radical leaders in the area, even though they have not embraced Communism. The Soviets expanded their support of and influence with Nasser when Dulles rudely broke off negotiations for the Aswan Dam. Khrushchev undertook to build the dam and support Nasser in 1956, even though he was putting the Egyptian Communists in jail. This must have upset some of the Party stalwarts in Moscow.

In the Middle East we seem to be in an unsolvable impasse, but I hope the Administration will continue to press for a solution. Patience and determination are needed where ill will is so intense. It's not an easy situation to deal with, and achieving a settlement is difficult.

Although we are deeply at odds with the Soviet Union in the Middle East, yet in the Subcontinent—India and Pakistan—we find ourselves in parallel positions. We are both trying to bring those two countries together to compose their differences, and we are both helping them economically. The Soviets are also providing substantial military assistance. The Russians clearly want to see India and Pakistan strong enough to resist Red China's advance to the south. And I am convinced that they have a similar desire in Southeast Asia.

This brings us to Vietnam.

Vietnam

I KNEW LITTLE ABOUT INDO-CHINA, except as a place on the map, until it began to be discussed during World War II. President Roosevelt several times in my presence said that the French would not be permitted back into Indo-China. This was in line with his pressure on Churchill for independence of India after the war and his belief that colonialism was on the way out. He sent an order to the Pentagon to make no plans about Indo-China. One of the tragic results of his early death was that he had not yet outlined the political moves he had in mind.

The British were given the responsibility of accepting the surrender of the Japanese in the southern part of Vietnam, and their divisional commander in Saigon turned it over to the French, apparently without high-level authorization. The French negotiated an agreement in 1946 with Ho Chi Minh for the independence of Vietnam within the French Union, but due to the arbitrary decision of the French authorities to shell Haiphong causing the death of many thousands of civilians, it fell through. All-out hostilities followed. That was a tragedy. An agreement on independence then would have saved the French and the Vietnamese a ghastly amount of effort, suffering, and lives, and it would have saved us as well.

Ho Chi Minh's regime might perhaps have become what could be called a "pre-Tito Asian Titoist" regime. Although a firm believer in Communism, Ho was a nationalist whose fundamental objective was independence for his country. He fought to end French colonialism. In 1919 he appealed to

President Wilson at Versailles to invoke his self-determination principle for Vietnam. He opposed any Chinese domination, as the Vietnamese had throughout history. By the postwar period he and the Viet Minh had established themselves in the eyes of most Vietnamese as the principal force for national independence. Furthermore, in his early public statements and in his contacts with Americans during the war Ho showed a friendly attitude toward the United States.

In retrospect, it seems possible that if a settlement had been made in the years following the war, Vietnam under Ho Chi Minh might well have been similar in some ways to Tito's Yugoslavia. It would have had its form of Communism internally, but might well have followed a foreign policy not dominated by Peking or Moscow and not unfriendly to the West—a policy which provided some counterweight to Chinese influence in the area.

That's where I began; I would like to end there. But unfortunately, we can't. First of all, it was a mistake to support the French in their attempt to maintain control. We tried to persuade them that they should grant independence to Indo-China and urged movement in that direction.

The French finally, in January 1950, did put into effect an agreement providing the Vietnamese with limited "self-government within the French Union" and, in form at least, handed over internal control to a regime headed by Emperor Bao Dai. Unfortunately, the fighting with Ho Chi Minh and the Viet Minh continued. Shortly thereafter we began providing economic and military supplies to the French for Vietnam. Under separate arrangements Cambodia and Laos were given their independence.

Of course, the Korean War came within a few weeks. When the Chinese entered the war, it seemed essential to help the French in Vietnam so as to divert some of China's effort from Korea.

Serious consideration was given in 1954 to military intervention in support of the French prior to the fall of Dienbienphu. This was supported by the Chairman of the Joint Chiefs, Admiral Radford; Secretary Dulles and Vice President Nixon. But President Eisenhower wisely insisted that congressional leaders be consulted and that support of our British allies be obtained. He found that neither would approve this proposed intervention, and he rejected it.

I can't imagine any sensible reason why Dulles took over from the French their role in South Vietnam in 1954. This was the basic decision which unwisely got us directly involved in South Vietnam. Under the 1954 Geneva Accords it was understood to be the French responsibility to give advice and support to South Vietnam. Instead of giving our aid to South Vietnam indirectly through the French as we had been, we now dealt directly with the newly established government of Ngo Dinh Diem and took over from the French political, economic, and military responsibility for that government. That started us down the road to our present involvement. You can be critical of subsequent steps that have been taken in expanding and escalating our involvement, but having once undertaken responsibility for South Vietnam, it was difficult to disengage.

When President Kennedy took office in January 1961 he faced an immediate crisis in Laos. The United States had been attempting to bolster a conservative political and military group in the government with economic and military assistance. The military were headed by General Phoumi Nosavan, a man we had backed. Political support came largely from the land-owning aristocrat class. Someone in authority in Washington had been quoted as saying that the United States objective was to make Laos a "bastion of Western strength."

However, Laos is a small country of about three and one half million peaceful people, whose territory cuts into the southern border of China and lies immediately to the west of North Vietnam. It is hard to understand how any United States policy makers could believe Laos could be successfully controlled by a government beholden to the United States, which Red China and North Vietnam would consider a direct threat. Looking back, a non-aligned, neutral, and non-Communist Laos might well have been acceptable to all, but in those days Secretary of State Dulles considered neutrality immoral.

In 1960 a neutralist government under Prince Souvanna Phouma took power, and our Ambassador in Laos strongly recommended that we accept it. However, General Phoumi who had military forces loyal to him in Southern Laos, was encouraged in late 1960 to advance on Vientiane. He ejected the government and set up a rightist regime under Prince Boun Oum. After General Phoumi's early successes in expanding the control of the new government he had been checked at the Plain of Jars by the combined forces of Souvanna Phouma's neutralists, joined by the Pathet Lao (Communists), and supported by North Vietnamese troops. For the first time Soviet arms were being supplied to these forces, expedited by an airlift. The military appraisal at the time President Kennedy took office in early 1961 indicated that without the intervention of outside troops, the rightist armies would be defeated and the capital of Vientiane could be taken within a few weeks.

President Kennedy rejected the idea of American military involvement in this faraway, land-locked country. Instead, he undertook to get agreement for a cease-fire and on the calling of a new international meeting of the countries concerned to settle the Laotian civil war. With the cooperation of the British and Russians, who as co-chairman of the 1954 Geneva conference had a continuing responsibility, he succeeded. A cease-fire was called for, and a meeting of fourteen interested countries was convened in early May in Geneva.

I personally was not involved in these early days. As Ambassador-at-Large I had been visiting, at the President's request, a number of European and other capitals to discuss our over-all relations. However, while in New Delhi, at Nehru's suggestion I had an informal talk with Prince Souvanna Phouma who happened to be there at the time. Later, the President asked me to handle the negotiations as the American delegate following the preliminary meetings attended by Foreign Ministers. From the beginning, President Kennedy made it unqualifiedly plain to me that he did not want to become involved militarily and that he wanted a compromise settlement which would permit Laos to become an independent and neutral country.

I wanted to visit Southeast Asia prior to the commencement of the conference but I had a very short time to do so. I had to make a fast-moving trip. In the eleven days away from Washington, I spent seven nights in seven different capitals— the other four on commercial airplanes. I met General Lemnitzer, Chairman of the Joint Chiefs of Staff, in Saigon. The situation of the side we were backing seemed so militarily weak that both of us recommended the positioning of American troops, at least temporarily, perhaps in Thailand to give some military strength from which to negotiate a compromise settlement. The President refused to do so at that time, but did so a year later, after a breakdown in the cease-fire.

On this trip I met Prince Souvanna Phouma again, in Pnom Penh. Based on the opinion of our Ambassador in Laos, Winthrop Brown, and French officials and my own conversations with him, I made up my mind early that a settlement must be worked out in some way around him. I found him to be a realistic patriot who wanted to see Laos develop as a non-aligned nation with normal and peaceful relations with its neighbors. Far from being a Communist as some State Department officers contended, he had a well-developed sense of the value of Western ideas gained from a French education. Let me add, this appraisal has been fully justified by Prince Souvanna Phouma's actions as Prime Minister over the past eight years.

This is not the place to recall the details of the long and tedious negotiations over the next fifteen months. These were not made easier by the opposition of some of our government officials who still held to the old thesis and even advised General Phoumi to hold out for unrealistic demands. Malcolm McDonald, the British delegate and co-chairman of the conference was a tower of strength, and I learned a lot about Soviet objectives in that area from Mr. Pushkin, Moscow's Deputy Foreign Minister and the other co-chairman. We could have had a somewhat more favorable agreement six or seven months earlier if it had not been for the opposition of General Phoumi. Whether this would have made much difference in the long run is now hard to say.

Throughout the period President Kennedy's position was unchanging. He fully supported the negotiations for a political settlement. In fact after one meeting with his advisers in late August, which I attended, he telephoned me personally to make sure I understood clearly his position. He said, "The alternative to an understanding with Souvanna is not one that I would like to contemplate."

Although he placed *temporarily* five thousand American troops in Thailand at a crucial moment in the spring of 1962 (they were withdrawn completely in two and a half months), he was determined to do all he could to avoid becoming directly involved in a military conflict. And he succeeded.

However, due to Pathet Lao intransigence and the North Vietnamese violations of the agreement, a *de facto* partition of the country has resulted. Most of the people of Laos have been living in the area controlled by Souvanna Phouma's government. He has attempted to maintain neutrality, but has asked our assistance when the North Vietnamese pressure on him became too great. In violation of the specific terms of the agreement, the North Vietnamese have continued to use the Ho Chi Minh Trail and have supported the Pathet Lao in order to achieve this objective.

Until the expansion of the war to Cambodia, I had hoped that a settlement of Vietnam would have permitted the re-establishment on a workable basis of the 1962 Laos agreement. Now a settlement of the Indo-Chinese war may well require at some point a new, multinational Geneva-type conference, including all the nations involved.

In South Vietnam, President Ngo Dinh Diem had been more successful in establishing control over more of the country in the late fifties than was first thought possible. By 1961, his position, however, was sharply deteriorating for two principal reasons. After no agreement was reached regarding the elections for reunification provided for in the 1954 Accords,[6] North Vietnam, in violation of those Accords, started to reactivate and reinforce the Viet Cong cadres left behind in South Vietnam. By 1961 guerrilla activity was threatening Diem's control of the country.

Second, Diem became more and more an arbitrary, mandarin-type ruler. He had abandoned the historic village elections of local officials as early as 1956, and he failed to carry out adequately his proposed land-reform program. He

[6] Evidence indicates both sides must share responsibility for this.

generally failed to gain the allegiance of the people. His position was undermined by the unpopular actions of his brother, Ngo Dinh Nhu, and his brother's wife. The Buddhists, students, and other non-Communist groups were beginning to protest. When President Kennedy took over, the situation was becoming increasingly unstable. Although the French were continuing to give some assistance in education, the Diem government was entirely dependent on the United States for military, political, and economic support. Before the end of 1961 the situation became so grave that President Kennedy sent a team of General Maxwell Taylor, Chairman of the Joint Chiefs of Staff, and Walt Rostow, White House Adviser, to review the situation and recommend action. They reported that further American involvement was essential if the Diem regime were to survive and a take-over by the Viet Cong avoided. On the basis of the recommendations of the Taylor-Rostow report, President Kennedy increased substantially our military advisers and supplied tactical air training and support but rejected the recommendation of direct military intervention with U.S. ground forces. At the time of his assassination two years later, American military personnel had risen to about sixteen thousand. Politically, conditions had continued to become increasingly unstable, with heightened demonstrations by the Buddhists and students.

There were already pessimistic reports from observers in South Vietnam in conflict with the overoptimism of our military command and our Embassy. I was present at one meeting when President Kennedy was receiving reports from two men recently sent to South Vietnam. Their reports were so different that the President with some annoyance asked, "Were you two gentlemen in the same country?"

Having seen this sort of thing over the years, I have become quite skeptical of reports out of Saigon. The conducted tours cannot help but be misleading. I thought George Romney might have the qualities of a good President when, after his return from Saigon he recognized that he had been taken in by his briefings. Unfortunately for his candidacy, he called it being "brainwashed," and that finished him.

The situation became so acute that Diem was forced out by a military coup on November 1, 1963. In the confusion of their capture, he and his brother were killed by a junior officer. These events deeply shocked President Kennedy.

It is too soon after the subsequent events for me to write about them in detail. Although it is not possible to say how President Kennedy would have handled Vietnam, it is my belief that he would never have become as heavily committed as we have. I believe that before he died he was already concerned that we were becoming too deeply involved.

I was then Under Secretary of State for Political Affairs, and shortly after President Johnson took over, he and Secretary of State Rusk asked me to give special attention to Africa, relieving me of my involvement in Vietnam. It was already obvious that my views on Vietnam were not well thought of in certain quarters. Africa, in which I was much interested, and other situations in the world kept me fully occupied.

I was glad to stay on, as my relations with President Johnson were cordial and continued to be so throughout his Administration. I had enormous admiration for his domestic policies. As a true disciple of President Roosevelt, he achieved social legislation on a wider front than any other President. To him these programs were unfinished business of the New Deal, with his own farsighted ideas of our social needs added. He told me more than once that he took the greatest satisfaction in the fact that he had tripled federal aid to education. He had never forgotten his early days as a school teacher.

He attacked with determination our critical problems. Civil

rights had to be achieved and achieved now. We had waited too long. Poverty had to be eliminated and all its causes attacked now. We had talked long enough about medical care for the aged, and action had to be taken now. Housing and community development appropriations were increased four-fold. He began to tackle our environmental problems, and Mrs. Johnson by her beautification program helped arouse nationwide concern about the desecration of our landscape. In the neglected field of the consumer, he employed for the first time a consumer adviser—the energetic and competent Esther Peterson—and got landmark legislation passed in consumer protection. I was particularly interested in his poverty, civil rights, and consumer programs as I had initiated new actions in these fields while I was Governor of New York.

I am not enumerating all his goals and achievements. Except for Roosevelt no President got so much going in so short a time. His initiatives have led to increasing public demands and inspired further action in all these fields. To me it is a tragedy that Vietnam was thrust upon him, which checked the fullest achievement of his enlightened objectives here at home.

Since Townsend Hoopes[7] and others have written about the difference in judgments among President Johnson's advisers, it's now possible to discuss the fact that, broadly speaking, there were two groups. I found myself in accord with Mr. McNamara who in December 1965, when the building of our forces in Vietnam had only reached two hundred thousand, was already for a political settlement rather than a military solution. His successor, Clark Clifford, has written in his own confessions (in *Foreign Affairs,* June 1969) that when he became Secretary of Defense in February 1968 he

[7] Former Under Secretary of the Air Force and author of *The Limits of Intervention.*

learned more about Vietnam and about the little interest the countries in the area showed in supplying troops to support our military action there. He quickly became an advocate of a bombing halt and a negotiated settlement. Together with Adlai Stevenson and his successor as Ambassador to the United Nations, Arthur Goldberg; George Ball and his successor as Under Secretary of State, Nicholas Katzenbach; there was a goodly group of people that were constantly pressing for that. I think it appropriate to let the others speak for themselves, but generally it is perhaps fair to say that they were hawks and believed our vital interests were at stake in South Vietnam in containing what they considered to be Red China's expansion in Asia.

During the last three years of President Johnson's administration, I was directly involved in his attempts to get negotiations going with Hanoi for a peaceful settlement. This started when the President called me on the telephone from the ranch at noon one day during Christmas week of 1965. He said, "Averell, have you got your bag packed?"

I replied, "It's always packed, sir. Where do you want me to go?"

He said, "There's a bombing halt, and I want you to talk with some of your Eastern European friends and see what they'll do."

I asked him whom he wanted me to see first, and he replied, "That's up to you. You know them better than I." He added: "Bob McNamara has a plane for you warming up at Andrews."

I didn't get much enthusiasm from Dean Rusk so I called Bob McNamara at the ranch for some advice. He explained in a bit more detail what the President had in mind. He wanted as many people as possible who had contact with Hanoi to impress on the North Vietnamese that the bombing had been suspended in the hope of getting negotiations started. The President called me a second time to make sure I understood that he didn't want anything or anyone to delay my leaving that day. He said, "You're reporting to me directly, as you've done before."

I made up my mind that it might embarrass the Soviet if I went directly to Moscow. Peking had been calling the Soviets agents of the United States. Also, Kosygin would be leaving for Tashkent shortly to mediate the Indian-Pakistan conflict. I knew Tito would always receive me but I thought it better to try Warsaw first. This guess turned out to be right. Poland was a member of the International Control Commission for Indo-China and thus had some involvement.

I sent a telegram to Ambassador Gronouski to get permission for my plane to land and hopefully to set up an appointment for me to see Foreign Minister Rapacki the next day. Due to the six hours difference in time, I had to leave that evening before getting an answer. I planned to stop off in Copenhagen if I didn't get a green light from Warsaw in time. As it turned out permission was granted, and I landed in Warsaw at three-thirty in the morning my time, nine-thirty o'clock Warsaw time.

Ambassador Gronouski met me at the airport with the news that Foreign Minister Rapacki would see me within the hour. I pled for a half hour's grace to go to the Embassy to wash up, have breakfast, and talk things over with the Ambassador. This proved no difficulty.

I found that Mr. Rapacki had set aside most of the day to talk with me. As he did not speak English we talked through an interpreter, which takes more time. But I have become accustomed to this, and I have found that there are distinct advantages to it. In the first place one gets a fuller record of the conversation. Then, too, there is less chance of being misunderstood and time to think about the way the conversation is developing. I explained in detail the President's position and gave him our fourteen-point basis for a settlement.[8]

He had with him several of his colleagues, including Deputy Foreign Minister Michalowski, now Polish Ambassador in Washington. He also took me to see Mr. Gomulka. As Secretary of the Communist Party, he was the leading force in the Polish government. I had known Mr. Gomulka in Moscow

[8] The fourteen points were:

1. The Geneva Agreements of 1954 and 1962 are an adequate basis for peace in Southeast Asia;
2. We would welcome a conference on Southeast Asia or on any part thereof;
3. We would welcome "negotiations without preconditions" as the seventeen nations put it;
4. We would welcome unconditional discussions as President Johnson put it;
5. A cessation of hostilities could be the first order of business at a conference or could be the subject of preliminary discussions;
6. Hanoi's four points could be discussed along with other points which others might wish to propose;
7. We want no U.S. bases in Southeast Asia;
8. We do not desire to retain U.S. troops in South Vietnam after peace is assured;
9. We support free elections in South Vietnam to give the South Vietnamese a government of their own choice;
10. The question of reunification of Vietnam should be determined by the Vietnamese through their own free decision;
11. The countries of Southeast Asia can be non-aligned or neutral if that be their option;
12. We would much prefer to use our resources for the economic reconstruction of Southeast Asia than in war. If there is peace, North Vietnam could participate in a regional effort to which we would be prepared to contribute at least one billion dollars;
13. The President has said, "The Viet Cong would not have difficulty being represented and having their views represented if for a moment Hanoi decided she wanted to cease aggression. I don't think that would be an unsurmountable problem."
14. We have said publicly and privately that we could stop the bombing of North Vietnam as a step toward peace although there has not been the slightest hint or suggestion from the other side as to what they would do if the bombing stopped.

during the war, as a member of the Polish partisans. He had come to my home in New York for a long personal talk in 1960 when he attended the United Nations summit meeting. No American official had seen him since then. In contrast to Mr. Rapacki's cordial manner, Gomulka was tough and critical, tactics to which I had become accustomed from talks with Stalin and other head Communist leaders. The Poles wanted to see the war stopped. Aside from the substantial cost of supplies to North Vietnam, which Moscow insisted Poland provide, I knew they were concerned about possible United States-Soviet confrontation over Vietnam. Their security would be jeopardized by any such clash.

I left Warsaw the following morning with assurances that the Poles would take some action, but I was not given any details. I subsequently learned that Michalowski had been dispatched to Moscow even before I left. He told me later that he had been well received there and encouraged to go on to Hanoi. He then went to Peking where he was met coldly and every attempt made to stop him. He proceeded anyway to Hanoi. He found the North Vietnamese leaders extremely skeptical. They were not prepared to enter negotiations at that time, probably because of Peking's influence. He felt, however, that he had made progress during his two weeks in Hanoi and his visit may have affected their subsequent attitudes. He told me that one of his difficulties was to convince the North Vietnamese of President Johnson's purpose and my authority to speak for him. They finally accepted his assurances based on his statement that Gomulka had been satisfied. Although some people have questioned it, I am convinced that the Polish government, and later the Romanian government, did everything they could to further negotiations.

I went on to see Tito and ran into a new difficulty—the

weather. He had asked me to come to his mountain hunting lodge at Brdo, but the nearby Ljubljana airport was closed down and, seemingly, so were all the other airports in Yugoslavia. After flying around Yugoslavia for some hours looking for a place open enough to come in, we finally landed at Belgrade in thick soup, thanks to our pilot's adroitness. From there we went by train overnight to Brdo, in Tito's diesel-powered private car. Tito, as always, received me cordially. I had known him since wartime days and then during the period after he had broken with Stalin. At President Truman's request I had visited him in 1951 to find out his military requirements. At the time he was afraid that Stalin would order an invasion of Yugoslavia. One interesting aspect of Tito's plan was that his military build-up was for defense against the neighboring satellite forces but not the Red Army. He stated flatly that Stalin would not engage the Red Army outside the Soviet Union or contiguous satellites.

During a long and cordial talk, Tito told me that he was most anxious to see the Vietnam war ended and agreed to urge Moscow to take advantage of Shelepin's visit to Hanoi to exert its influence in favor of negotiations.[9] In fact he called in the Soviet Ambassador that same afternoon. He told me, however, that he could be of no help with Peking. He said that they directed their harshest attacks at him. He explained that a few days before they had "called me a revisionist bandit." I commented that that was not so bad, as Peking had called us "imperialist bandits" for years. Tito replied, "You don't understand. A 'revisionist bandit' is far worse a character than an 'imperialist bandit.'"

[9] Alexander Shelepin was a member of the Politburo and Secretary of the Central Committee of the Communist Party. At the time he was in Hanoi with a high-ranking delegation including military and economic experts.

I hurried on to New Delhi as I wanted to see Prime Minister Shastri and then President Ayub in Pakistan before they left to meet with Chairman Kosygin in Tashkent. India had a special interest in Vietnam as it was the Chairman of the International Control Commission. Mr. Shastri saw me on my arrival as he was leaving for Tashkent the next day. He told me that he warmly "welcomed the President's move" and assured me that he would do everything he could to encourage Hanoi to negotiate and would "undertake to talk to Kosygin." He explained that he had felt for some time that the Soviets wanted peace, whereas Peking wanted the fighting to continue. Unfortunately, Prime Minister Shastri died of a heart attack while in Tashkent, but I heard from his associates that he had carried out his agreement and had talked at some length with Mr. Kosygin on this subject.

Next day I caught President Ayub at the Peshawar airport just before he left for Tashkent. After a detailed discussion, he agreed with President Johnson's position including our fourteen points. He assured me he would do what he could with Kosygin but doubted if he could do much with Peking. Like Shastri, he expressed the belief that the Kremlin wanted the fighting ended, while Peking felt it was to their interest to have the war continue. He urged the President to be patient. "We are dealing with strange people who have been at war a long time," he said. "It may take time for them to make up their minds."

At Tito's suggestion I went on to Cairo to see Nasser. He was one of the seventeen neutralist leaders who had recently called for negotiations. I asked him to use his influence with Hanoi and Peking and induce the other neutralists to do the same. Nasser stated categorically, "We want peace," but maintained that it would take time, perhaps three or four months, to get negotiations started. He urged restraint and a continuation of the bombing pause. "The United States is a great power," he said, "and can afford to be patient."

He described his talks with Chou En-lai in which Chou adamantly opposed negotiations. Nasser said he believed Peking considered the continuation of the war to be in their interest, but that the Soviet Union was "more moderate and wanted a peaceful solution." He received me in his home on the evening of my arrival and showed real interest in our discussion of the problem and what he might do. The next morning I called on Foreign Minister Riad, who had been present at my talk with Nasser. He told me that they would talk with the Hanoi representative and later the Chinese. What came of these talks I have never known.

In addition I visited on this trip Iran, Thailand, Japan, Australia, Laos, South Vietnam, and the Philippines. I found that President Johnson's initiative was widely welcomed by the governments, in contrast with the skepticism of some press reports. I talked with the heads of state or government, and in every case they offered to cooperate in some appropriate way. Unfortunately, these efforts and those stimulated by other American ambassadors were not successful in obtaining a favorable reaction from Hanoi. The North Vietnamese were not yet prepared to negotiate a settlement and reportedly still hoped for a victory like the one over the French at Dienbienphu. They were probably influenced by Peking who wanted the fighting to continue. The Russians, I believe, were already recommending negotiations. The bombing was therefore resumed following Tet, on January 31, after a thirty-seven-day pause.

A few months later President Johnson asked me to take special responsibility for following closely all possible peace leads. Although I didn't think justly, the Administration was being accused of missing signals from Hanoi that could have been profitably followed up. By this time I had resigned as Under Secretary for Political Affairs, and the President had asked me to stay on as Ambassador-at-Large to undertake special assignments. For instance, I had visited eight Latin American countries to discuss the Dominican crisis with the heads of state.

In attempting to carry out this new responsibility, I added one man to my staff—a colleague whom I felt was particularly qualified—Chester Cooper. He had been a member of the White House staff and had long experience with Indo-China, including both the 1954 and 1962 Geneva Conferences. When, a year later, he had to leave to carry out other commitments, I was fortunate to get Daniel Davidson, a young lawyer working as a special assistant to William Bundy, Assistant Secretary of State for the Far East, to take his place. Instead of building a large separate staff, for which I have an aversion, the two of us used all the facilities of the State Department and other agencies to assist us.

A number of potential leads developed, the most promising of which came from Romania. I visited Bucharest in December 1967 on my way back from Pakistan, where I had represented the President at the opening ceremonies of the great Indus River Mangla Dam. In Bucharest I had several long talks with Prime Minister Maurer who had been to Hanoi and gave me a detailed account of his conversations there. I also had an interesting talk with Mr. Ceausescu, the Secretary of the Communist Party. As a result, Deputy Foreign Minister Macovescu made two trips to Hanoi and reported to us in Washington in the interim. Although nothing immediate came from this initiative, I cannot help feeling that the discussions carried on by the Romanians contributed to Hanoi's ultimate decision to start the talks in Paris. In any event we have every reason to appreciate the unusual effort and meticulous care with which the Romanians tried to get negotiations going.

There is going to be a lot written about who influenced the President to make his offer of March 1968 to limit our bombing to the panhandle of North Vietnam, combined with the announcement of his decision not to seek re-election. For my part, there is just one man who influenced President Johnson and that was President Johnson himself.

As Townsend Hoopes records, Nick Katzenbach and I came independently to the conclusion that a total halt of the bombing was necessary and that it should take place toward the end of April. I was influenced by Ambassador Bunker's feeling that President Thieu needed one month more to re-establish the stability of his government in the aftermath of the Tet offensive. I had determined to make as strong a case as I could personally to the President for a complete cessation of the bombing at that time. With the approaching election campaign I felt strongly that this would be about the last chance the President would have without being accused of playing domestic politics. Of course, I assumed he would run for re-election. From the general atmospherics coming out of Hanoi, I also believed this would be a propitious moment. Although I was glad to see any move toward negotiations, I did not believe that a limited halt in the bombing would be sufficient to get Hanoi to agree to come to a conference.

The prompt and favorable reply that came from Hanoi seemed to confirm the fact that Hanoi had an initiative in mind following the Tet offensive. Charles Collingwood, the CBS correspondent, and other foreigners in Hanoi had gained this impression from talks with senior North Vietnam officials. Looking back, I still believe it would have been better to have stopped the bombing completely on the basis of the San Antonio formula.[10] This would have permitted many months for substantive negotiations rather than the tedious wrangle about conditions or circumstances which would permit a total bombing cessation. I firmly believe there would have been a good chance to have made real progress toward a peaceful settlement during President Johnson's Administration, and the military situation left to the new Administration would have been at least a reduced level of combat, possibly a cease-fire and a substantial number of our forces on the way home.

Hanoi has objected to discussing the withdrawal of their troops with us, contending that this was a matter for the Vietnamese to settle among themselves. However, I feel sure that mutual withdrawals could have been carried out on the basis of mutual example even though Hanoi would have resisted making a formal agreement on a schedule. But all this is speculative.

Negotiations with the North Vietnamese began in Paris on May 10, 1968. The President asked Cy Vance and me to handle them.[11] Cy was more than a Deputy, he was my partner throughout the long and frustrating months. And no one could have had a better one. We were fortunate, too, in the other members of our mission and our staff.

As it was, after nearly six months' discussion, President Johnson was able to stop the bombing at the end of October

[10] In President Johnson's speech on September 29, 1967, at San Antonio, he stated: "The United States is willing to stop all aerial and naval bombardment of North Vietnam when this will lead promptly to productive discussions. We, of course, assume that while discussions proceed, North Vietnam would not take advantage of the bombing cessation or limitation."

[11] Cyrus R. Vance had been Secretary of the Army, 1962–63 and then Deputy Secretary of Defense until 1967. He had also undertaken troubleshooting assignments for President Johnson in Cyprus, Korea, and during the summer riots of 1967. He was at the time a member of the New York law firm of Simpson, Thacher & Bartlett.

1968. President Thieu had been kept constantly informed of all of our discussions through his mission in Paris and our Embassy in Saigon. Throughout this period he had never indicated that he was not willing to join the talks in Paris. We had considerable difficulty in getting the other side to agree to negotiate with his representative. They seemed to have a special bitterness toward Thieu as they had been fighting him for years, way back to the French colonial period, when they considered him a mercenary of the French.

For our part, we refused to accept the NLF as independent participants. We maintained they were creatures of Hanoi. We finally settled on a compromise which satisfied both sides, including Thieu, we believed. There were, of course, two sides to the negotiations, but each side would have the right to include anyone it wanted. The North Vietnamese informed us the NLF would participate on their side, and we informed them the Saigon government would participate on ours. We called it "two-sided," while they called it "four-party." However, it was understood that neither of us would challenge the other's interpretation. We devised this unique arrangement to overcome the resistance of Thieu, to accepting the NLF as independent of the North Vietnamese, and the other side's refusal to recognize Thieu's regime as the government of South Vietnam.

Then, much to President Johnson's surprise (we were aghast in Paris), at the last moment Thieu refused.

We had been working intensively with the North Vietnamese in Paris for the prior two weeks on the specifics of how and when President Johnson could stop the bombing of the North and the substantive negotiations for a peaceful settlement could begin. In accordance with President Johnson's instructions, we had finally reached an agreement.

Clark Clifford in his press conference of November 12, 1968, gave an account of what happened on October 29 and the following days. His account conforms to the way we saw things from Paris. I was relieved that he spoke out at that time, as it cleared the atmosphere of innuendoes critical of President Johnson coming out of Saigon. I am sure Clifford did so to protect President Johnson. From the days of President Truman I have known him to be a most careful, precise, and loyal colleague. To help clear the atmosphere now, I quote from the transcript of his press conference at length as follows:

Question: Sir, would you speak to the charges made . . . that the Administration knew, before they made the bombing halt and the announcement of the agreement on the 31, that the South Vietnamese government would not go along with the talks in Paris. And also would you speak to whether you think the South Vietnamese government has been dealt very brusquely with. . . .

Secretary Clifford: We started the talks with Hanoi in May. Those talks have gone on and went on for some five and one half months, all during that time, Ambassador Bunker was kept fully informed of all developments in Paris. He, in turn, kept President Thieu fully informed. . . . He knew what our goal was. He knew that we were working for a kind of an arrangement that would enable us to get on with the talks.

Now, keep in mind that during this period, it was the government in Saigon that was insisting . . . that they had to be present at the conference table in Paris, and we took that position with Hanoi. Hanoi had said consistently . . . they were not going to permit the "imperialist puppets" to be present at the conference table in Paris. This was one of the major reasons for the deadlock. . . . We thought they should be at the table. Now, also, in addition to that, Saigon was kept fully posted on what the other arrangements were that we were working toward; that is, some understanding about the DMZ; an understanding with reference to the cities. We [also had] talks having to do with reconnaissance. They were kept fully informed. And Thieu came along and Ky came along on all these talks. They understood every single question that had come up.

They agreed with us when we got to the middle of October that there had been a breakthrough when Hanoi sent us the message through their negotiators in Paris and asked us the question: "If we, Hanoi, were to agree to the presence of the Saigon government, could this constitute real progress?"

We said at once, "Yes, it could constitute real progress in the talks, but it isn't everything. For the talks to go on, we have to have this kind of understanding about the cities and about the DMZ."

We kept Thieu fully informed, and it got down to the point where even a joint announcement or a communique was prepared that stated what the arrangement was. . . . All it left blank was the date that the bombing was to [stop and the date the meeting was] to be held, at which the Saigon government was to be present. It even got down to the point where, in the communique that had been agreed on, they asked that in the Saigon version that . . . the GVN, be mentioned first and the United States be mentioned second.

All through this period, it was clearly understood beyond any question whatsoever that the NLF would accompany the government in Hanoi to the conference table, and it was known that the Saigon government would accompany the United States. Now, when finally [General Creighton] Abrams came back, on the early morning of Tuesday, October 29, we spent some three hours with him. He said not only did he feel there was an acceptable military risk in stopping the bombing and going on, he said, "Mr. President, I recommend this course of action." The Joint Chiefs had recommended it, all of which also had been imparted to Mr. Thieu and his senior advisers.

Then all that we had to do on that Tuesday was to fill in on this agreed upon communique . . . the date of the cessation of the bombing and the date of the first talk. We broke up that meeting on Tuesday morning with the sure knowledge—I did—that finally we had arrived at the end of this journey that had taken some five and one half months. We were all to go to bed and get some rest. Then the President was going on the air that night, Tuesday night, the twenty-ninth of October, and make his speech and announce that he was stopping the bombing that night, because that was the date [agreed to with the North Vietnamese] and that he was going to meet with the other side and with the GVN in Paris on Saturday, the second of November.

Later that day we were working on the speech, we got the first word from Thieu that he couldn't go along with the arrangement . . . that had been agreed on for weeks. . . . And also, and this is most interesting, the only reason that Thieu gave that he couldn't go along with this deal was because he said he didn't have time to get his delegation to Paris by Saturday, November 2. That was the only reason that he gave.

So we have to then consider—should we extend the date? Should we try to talk again? Sure, they can get there by the second. So cables have to go back and forth again.

Then the next day, Wednesday, the thirtieth, that one reason which had been time only, had expanded into some four or five reasons, every one of which would cause very substantial delay in the Saigon government getting to Paris. For instance, they said, "Well, we have a lot of procedural questions that have to be ironed out beforehand." That hadn't been brought up before. "Also, this problem about whether or not Hanoi will talk independently to us. That's got to be worked out first." "Also, we have decided we must bring back our Ambassador in Paris and talk to him." That hadn't been mentioned before. That obviously would take quite a lot of time.

So here came a whole new set of concerns and objections, every one of which would consume a substantial amount of time. Then talks are held by Bunker and Thieu on Wednesday.

Then we go over to Thursday, the thirty-first of October. Now the President has a very tough problem at this time. He had a deal with Hanoi in Paris. He had worked on it for six months. He had finally said, "Right, we've now got it to the point where I can accept it." He was committed. I felt that he was committed, and he felt that he had to go ahead on his commitment. So on Thursday we informed the government in Saigon that the President had this commitment and that he was going ahead and announce that night that he was stopping the bombing the next morning, Friday, November 1, and that the talks would take place on the sixth of November, which would give them plenty of time to meet their first objection.

He was still hopeful on that day, Thursday, that we'd still get word. We kept the sentence open as to how we would treat the GVN. In the earlier draft of the speech, we had that the meeting would take place on such-and-such a date and that the GVN would be present. Well, we had to wait. Finally, toward the afternoon when the tape had to be cut, we said to change it: that the GVN would be free to be present. There was still hope that we would hear from them on Thursday that they would. Then there was still hope that these problems that had been brought up at the last minute would be ironed out by the sixth of November, so that they could participate in the meeting. But by the time the sixth of November came, they said no; they could not participate.

Now here is the position the President was in on Thursday—and I might say I feel it strongly because I see what he had to go through. He worked through five and one half months to reach an agreement that he thought could be a major step toward peace, and then in the last out of the ninth inning, why suddenly they say, "No, we can't go along." I think the President felt he had to proceed with his plan. He was committed. He had made the commitment to Hanoi. Vance and Harriman had put their word on the line, and I think he felt he had to go ahead. In addition to that, after all that we have done in that country, after the enormous contribution that's been made, with the knowledge that we had gotten to the point where we had the sort of agreement that we had been working toward, I believe the President was absolutely right in not giving Saigon a veto on the plan.

I do not believe that . . . you can work along with your partner up to this . . . very last instant, with the understanding full and complete as to what the arrangement is, and then suddenly have Saigon change its mind and decide not to go ahead. I think the President owed it, under his constitutional duty, I think he owed it to the American people to proceed with the talks.

Now, I say that I believe we should make reasonable effort to demonstrate to Saigon why it should come in and join the talks. At the same time, if they choose not to, I believe the President has the constitutional responsibility of proceeding with the talks.

There are a great many subjects that can be covered between the United States and Hanoi of a military nature and that's our real function. We have been there as a military shield for South Vietnam. I have not anticipated that we would get into the political settlement of South Vietnam. That is up to South Vietnam and Hanoi. But we can work out arrangements with Hanoi in Paris that could be very valuable. We could work out steps that could lead to a diminution in the level of the combat, which we all desire very much. I would like to see our casualties go down. I believe we can work out arrangements in that regard. I believe that we can sit down with Hanoi and begin to work out programs that would call for the withdrawal, both of North Vietnamese forces and of American forces.

So the President has all this in his mind when he has to make that decision on Thursday. I say to you that I felt that he acted with courage and he acted with forthrightness, and I don't know when I have ever been as proud of a President as I was of President Johnson on Thursday when he had to face up to this question with all the political implications and pressures that were bearing on him. Mind you, he did not pick the day to announce this. This had been brought about by the decision on the part of Hanoi. . . . When the offer was made and the offer was accepted, it was up to the President to proceed with it because the opportunity of ending the war was of infinitely greater importance than any possible political consideration.

Question: Mr. Secretary, do you think that there should have been a notification of Mr. Nixon with regard to this great problem that they were having with South Vietnam, or do you think that was kind of glided over in the conversations the President had with Nixon and the other candidates at that stage?

Secretary Clifford: Well, I happened to be there in the President's office when President Johnson talked to candidates Nixon, Humphrey, and Wallace. It was a talk that came through the open box so that we could hear not only what the President said, but we could hear what the other side said. Secretary Rusk was there. General Wheeler was there. Mr.

Rostow was there, and I was there. We had just been through the matter with the President. We then went into his office, and he talked to the three candidates. He told the three candidates at that time, as clearly as I am telling you now, this story. . . . He shortened it a good deal, but he gave them the salient facts. He told them that up until Tuesday morning that Saigon had been right with us. He told them at that time that they had raised objections and that we were in contact with them, that they were not at the time aboard, as I remember the quote, but that we still hoped that by the sixth of November they would be. They were informed at that time specifically by the President that we had run into this snag by Saigon.

Question: Mr. Secretary, if you had to do it over again, do you think there would be any validity in the suggestion that has been offered that for terms of American unity, the announcement of the bombing halt should have been made after the election so it would not have had an impact right in the closing days of the election? What would have been lost?

Secretary Clifford: You asked me for my opinion on it. I would have done it. I don't wish to be presumptuous, but I would have done it as the President did it. I think that when you reach an agreement after all these months of work, that you finally have even the dates set with Hanoi in Paris—keeping mind that the timing and the dates was a question of considerable importance. At one time, Hanoi wanted a very long period between the cessation of the bombing and the start of the substantive talks. We wanted a very short one. We wanted twenty-four hours.

They wanted a very long period. We go back and forth, back and forth, every decision being made by the President, and Harriman and Vance acted upon the instructions of the President.

We go all through this process. We finally get down to the point where there is a solid agreement then on the dates. I believe the President had a responsibility to proceed with the agreement that he made, and he had to do it no matter what the effect might be, as I said before, because I think the importance of the talks in getting on with those efforts which could end the war, far transcended in importance whatever some political result might be.

Question: Mr. Secretary, what went wrong? . . .

Secretary Clifford: I cannot speculate on what came up that caused the government in Saigon to change its mind. I know only that the understanding was as clear as two partners can have, over a substantial period of time. I know that Tuesday morning we had an understanding. I know by Tuesday afternoon they raised this first [objection]. . . .

There seems to be little doubt that through one channel or another Thieu was counseled to wait until after the American election. He was evidently told Nixon would be much harder-line than Humphrey, and he was warned that if negotiations began, Humphrey might be elected.

I don't in any way suggest that President Nixon knew anything about this. But some believe that if we had started actual negotiations during the week before election day, it might well have made the small, but vital difference in the outcome of the election. If Hubert Humphrey had been elected President, we would have been well out of Vietnam by now. I can say this with assurance because I am satisfied he would have appointed either George Ball or Clark Clifford his Secretary of State, and I know where they stood.

During the period between the election and inauguration, we worked hard to get negotiations going. I am not very good at making a case for the enemy, but the North Vietnamese did disengage in the two northern provinces of I Corps. That had been an area of some of the bloodiest fighting involving Americans—Khesanh and the like. The North Vietnamese had a large force there. They took 90 per cent of their troops out, and half of them above the 20th Parallel, some two hundred miles to the north. There was almost complete disengagement, so much so that it permitted General Abrams to take the 1st Air Cavalry Division out of I Corps to the III Corps for increased action there.

It seemed clear to us that this was an invitation to reduce the level of fighting and perhaps work toward a cease-fire. During that time Clark Clifford made several public statements that the first order of business when substantive negotiations began should be the reduction in the level of combat. Cy Vance and I fully agreed that this might be achieved either by mutual example or specific agreement. I used the phrase level of "violence" as well as combat, as I included the Viet Cong terrorist actions.

I felt the B-52s were an important negotiating weapon. Although the North Vietnamese never admitted the damage done, they did describe to us in Paris the terrific effect on morale of hell breaking loose from the sky without warning. I felt that in return for the stopping of B-52 raids, they might well agree to stop their terrorist activities at least in the cities, and their ambushing along the principal highways. From the North Vietnamese actions as well as what they said, I believed that had substantive negotiations begun in early

November as had been agreed to, definite progress in reducing the level of combat could have been made permitting some of our troops to start home that year (1968). Instead, even after President Thieu agreed to permit his representatives to join the talks in Paris, there was that undignified row about the table. The North Vietnamese were willing to accept a round table which we in Paris had recommended. Historically that has always been the way to avoid questions of protocol. Thieu refused, however, for the simple reason that he did not want to have any substantive discussions before President Nixon came in. In fact, he tried to break up the talks entirely until, as I understand it, President-elect Nixon sent word to Thieu that he wanted the talks to continue. But due to the help of the Soviets, Hanoi did accept a table arrangement almost the same as one Saigon had proposed, and so, with the patience and skill of Cy Vance, all the procedural arrangements were settled at the very end, just before January 20. Substantive negotiations for a peaceful settlement were now, at long last, ready to begin. Yet, nothing constructive happened.

Before I go on, I want to point out that some people say the Russians won't help us out of Vietnam. I can say they did help us—in October 1968. That is a fact. And they helped in January 1969 too. They didn't stop the war. They have only limited influence with Hanoi, but when we are moving toward an agreement, they can be of considerable help and can remove roadblocks.

They can, I think, add some confidence to Hanoi in its negotiations and help allay its suspicions. Hanoi felt it had an agreement with the French in 1946, you remember, and that petered out. The North Vietnamese also think the 1954 Geneva Accords were not carried out as they were intended.

But the Soviets won't try to force North Vietnam to accept our dictates. They look upon North Vietnam as what they call a "sister" Communist state. They feel they have an obligation as the great leader of the Communist "camp" to support them. That is their attitude. I don't defend it, but I am explaining their point of view.

When I left Paris in January 1969, we had arranged that the two sides, with two on each side, would sit down privately and talk together. There is no doubt in my mind that President Thieu scuttled those negotiations, and he did it consciously. He announced on January 29 that he was not going to sit down in private, and one of his spokesmen said, "Whatever we have got to tell the Communists we have already told them in Paris, and it is not necessary to have private meetings with them." This was, of course, nonsense, because they knew that we got nowhere in those public discussions and that whatever progress was made had to be done privately. So there were no private talks among the four.

Our formal meetings were held at the Hotel Majestic, an official building of the French government. Although the press was not admitted, these meetings were thoroughly publicized. Each side gave out its prepared statement and then briefed the press on the rebuttals. However, first at our suggestion, the Vietnamese representatives joined us at the tea breaks—thirty- to forty-minute recesses during the lengthy meetings. We broke up into four or five separate small groups in the different reception rooms. This gave our delegates and staff members a chance to chat with their opposite numbers. Unfortunately, the tea break talks did not continue after January 20, 1969.

These informal talks proved to be of considerable value in helping to understand each other's ideas and attitudes. The sort of thing that came up naturally was a discussion of miracle rice, which we had referred to in our formal statement. The Vietnamese showed a keen interest as they obviously want to increase rice production to end the need for imports.

Our private meetings were conducted in secret by special arrangement. We held many of them over the months in secluded places. Although it became known to the press that there were private talks, no one knew when or where we met. Nor was there a leak from either side of a word we discussed.

My partner, Cy Vance, stayed on in Paris for a month under the new Administration, and during that period Ambassador Lodge had no private talks on substantive matters. I understand he didn't attempt to have such private talks for two months. By that time Thieu had "graciously" stated that he would sit down privately with the other side, but the chain was broken. Thieu had stated at the same time that in no circumstances would he agree to a coalition government and under no circumstances would he agree to permit a Communist party in South Vietnam. These were prior conditions which the other side would not take. So that action by Thieu blocked progress in Paris.

Why should we give Thieu the right to dictate American policy? I can't conceive why anybody should give a veto to a foreign potentate, no matter who he is.

We should want to stop this fighting in Vietnam. To me the Vietnamization of the war is an immoral thing. We have no right to perpetuate the fighting. Every effort should be made to end the human tragedy that is going on in South Vietnam.

Our political objectives in Vietnam cannot be achieved by military means. We can expand the war to include Cambodia,

Laos, North Vietnam, and then China, and even the Soviet Union, but this war cannot be won. That is not the fault of the United States but the nature of the problem that exists there.

Unfortunately, this Administration has not concentrated its attention on negotiations but rather on military action.

On April 20, 1970, the President held out hope that a "just peace" was in sight, yet ten days later the war was expanded. There seems to be an idea that military blows can force the other side to negotiate on our terms. All our past experience in Vietnam shows that this is a delusion.

The Administration's program of Vietnamization of the war is not in my opinion a program for peace but is a program for the perpetuation of the war. At best, we can only hope for a reduction of less than half of our forces in South Vietnam two and a half years after this Administration took office. But after that there is no assurance whether or when the balance of our forces will be withdrawn. The South Vietnamese troops are able to take on more of the load of our combat troops, but there is no indication that they can continue to operate successfully without American air, artillery, and logistic support.

Furthermore, the Vietnamization of the war is dependent on an unpopular and repressive military government. With all of the military influence, President Thieu and Vice President Ky got less than 35 per cent of the votes cast in 1967, whereas over 60 per cent of the votes were cast for civilian candidates who had some kind of peace plank in their platform. This election confirmed the judgment that the people of South Vietnam want peace and not a continuation of the war.[12]

The senatorial elections in August 1970 give further evidence of the desire of the people for the ending of the war. The

[12] Extracted from testimony before the House Foreign Affairs Committee, May 25, 1970.

anti-war Buddhist slate, headed by Vu Van Mau, which reportedly emphasized peace through compromise, was among the three slates elected. It got more votes than even the leading pro-government slate backed by the government and the military. It is significant also that the other pro-government slates were beaten. The third winning group was anti-government on domestic issues.

I said on several occasions in Paris with the approval of Washington that the United States was against imposition of a government on the people of South Vietnam either by Hanoi or Washington. I must say I stated that hoping it would have an influence in the United States as well as in North Vietnam. But now we find we are trying to impose this military regime on the people of South Vietnam. It is common knowledge that Thieu is putting a number of his opposition in jail—even a member of the Lower House, Tran Ngoc Chau, in violation of his constitutional immunity. Thieu met President Nixon at Midway Island in June 1969, and the first thing he did when he came home was announce that he was going to punish severely anyone that proposed a coalition government with the NLF. President Nixon had said that he was not going to impose a coalition government, that it was up to the South Vietnamese to work out their own future themselves—with a coalition government if they chose.

From the beginning the Johnson Administration had urged Thieu and Ky to broaden their government to include representatives of all the non-Communist political elements. In the spring of 1968, after the Tet offensive and President Johnson's partial bombing halt, Thieu brought in as Premier Tran Van Houng, a civilian and former presidential candidate. Thieu seemed to be making an effort to broaden his government and increase his popular support in preparation for serious negotiation. However, after the meeting with President Nixon at Midway Island, he accepted Houng's resignation and he replaced him with a close, loyal military officer, General Khiem. He abandoned any attempt to make the government more broadly representative and he tightened his military control of the government and its policies.

It is hard to envision a satisfactory solution unless Thieu does what we have tried to get him to do since 1967, broaden his government. He should rally the non-Communist forces, form an alliance representative of the majority of the people of South Vietnam. Big Minh, who was the most popular of the generals, is in this mood. I have talked to Senator Don, who was also a general, but is now a leader of the opposition in the Senate. The Buddhists, the Cao Dai, Hoa Hao, the labor unions, and other non-Communist groups must be brought in. (Thieu himself is a Catholic.) They are anxious to have an end to the war. They want to stay in their country. They know that a military victory can't be won, and they are ready to make a political settlement. But they need to organize together so as to be able to win the political contest which will come after the end of hostilities. That is what we ought to be concentrating on.

If we wait passively until the present Saigon government fields a team that wants a settlement, we won't make progress in Paris or anywhere else. Also, it seems quite obvious to everyone that President Nixon, in fact, downgraded negotiations. He said that he wants to negotiate. However, he left in Paris a very good Foreign Service officer who is a friend of mine, but who was third in rank to me and then to Lodge. On the other hand, the NVN are represented by a man who was Foreign Minister, and the "adviser," Le Duc Tho, is a high-ranking member of their Politburo. The negotiations were to have been on that senior level. The President should appoint a successor for Lodge who has the same prestige and position that Lodge had.[13]

All our troops should be withdrawn from Vietnam—on a prompt, announced schedule as proposed by former Secretary of Defense Clark Clifford. This will compel the Thieu government to undertake seriously negotiations for a responsible settlement. He must bring into his government the political elements desiring peace and send to Paris a team willing and capable of negotiating with the NLF for a compromise solution. If this is done, I believe the other side will join in serious negotiations.

The assurance from us that we intended to remove our troops completely from South Vietnam is necessary to get the North Vietnamese to negotiate a reasonable compromise. Obviously, if Hanoi was recalcitrant, the President, I would hope in consultation with the Senate, could hold up the withdrawal schedule.

Our withdrawal should be responsible, and I believe that it can be—without delaying the return of our troops. We helped set this country on fire, and we must help put it out. I am convinced that the other side will agree to one point at least—that there will be no reprisals by either side, with supervision by an international body. Also, we must arrange for the prompt return of all our men who are prisoners of war. Other issues must be subject to negotiation among the Vietnamese themselves.

In the many private discussions I had with the North Viet-

[13] In July 1970 President Nixon filled the position with the excellent appointment of the veteran diplomat, Ambassador David Bruce. He also made new proposals for a peaceful settlement in October 1970.

namese in Paris, there is one thing that I learned. They are fiercely nationalistic. They particularly want to be independent of China. With this in mind, they established friendly relations with the French after the war with France ended. Now if our war can be ended, they want similar relations with the United States. Like Tito, they recognize the need for an alternative to being compelled to rely on their powerful Communist neighbor.

I therefore believe that it is important for us to come to an understanding with Hanoi. We must recognize that the North Vietnamese did not keep the Laos agreement of 1962 for a single day and some understanding must be reached which is to their interest to keep for a period of years. If we are to have peace in Southeast Asia, some understanding must be arrived at along the lines of President Johnson's Johns Hopkins speech of April 1965 for the reconstruction and regional development, with the participation of the North Vietnamese.

Events have made this more difficult. Peking has consistently taken a negative position on a peaceful solution in the area. Peking's influence, I believe, was at its lowest point in 1968. However, developments following the overthrow of Sihanouk and our intervention in Cambodia have increased their position to a new high.

An attempt on our part to support pro-Western military governments in the area regardless of local opposition is quite impossible of permanent achievement without the continued presence of large United States forces in Vietnam and a perpetuation of the fighting. Aside from North Vietnam, these countries are so close to the Chinese border that this policy is provocative and would be interpreted by Red China as a threat to its security. I believe if we would look at the area dispassionately, we could not avoid the conclusion that non-aligned, neutral governments are the best we can expect and are in the long run compatible with our interests.[14]

We have been told that "our will and character" are being tested in world opinion by our actions in Indo-China. That is not correct. What is being tested is our judgment and the wisdom of our purpose.[15]

Here at home I believe student unrest and the generation gap were given impetus by disillusion over Vietnam. In the view of many students, if the older generations could be so unwise and unmoral about this war, they must be basically responsible for other wrongs in our society.

I am not suggesting that if the war was stopped tomorrow, it would end campus unrest, but it would be the first important step in that direction. Unhappily, President Nixon has scorned student opinion on Vietnam, and this has led to increased campus tensions and has tended to draw the more responsible students toward the extremists involved in anti-war demonstrations.

It is easy to be destructive. I reject the rock throwers and the burners. They not only destroy, but their excesses play into the hands of the most reactionary. However, I have profound respect for the students who are taking constructive action.

I readily gave my support to the Moratorium in New York. I believe John Lindsay's participation in the Moratorium was a turning point in his campaign for mayor. When people talk

[14] We should not confuse Indo-China with South Korea, which is quite a different situation. In South Korea we have had United Nations participation and support. South Korea is a peninsular with a relatively short border with North Korea to defend. It has no indigenous subversive organization. It has been able to develop a strong government with a flourishing economy and a vigorous military force. In addition it lies within 125 miles of Japan's largest island and has close economic relations with that country.

[15] Extracted in part from Commencement Address at Georgetown University, June 7, 1970.

about the lack of support the students have, when President Nixon says he will disregard their opinions, Lindsay evidently felt they spoke for a lot of people. So on Moratorium Day, October 15, 1969, he addressed one hundred thousand people gathered in Union Square, and I think that is one of the reasons why people suddenly reappraised this man and his capacity for leadership. Maybe it was that. If it wasn't that, maybe it was because the Mets won the championship! The polls showed the improvement in his popularity at that time.

In any event, the Moratorium was a thrilling experience—the job that was done by the students in organizing and exercising control was first-rate. However, I publicly opposed the New Mobilization March on Washington in November. I felt it would be counter-productive. The group that organized it included extremists and advocates of violence—the kind of people whose involvement always damages a good cause.

I hope that the students will rally and work constructively in the coming campaign to bring out as many people as possible, and show President Nixon what the great silent majority really thinks. The reality of the situation is that we have wasted many months. The tragedy of lost American lives, the tragedy of the division of our country, the tragedy of the diversion of resources that we ought to be applying to the many urgent needs in this country should be brought to an end.

★　★　★

Q   Governor Harriman, is there any credibility to the rumor that American casualties in Vietnam have been systematically understated?

WAH   I don't believe so; I am satisfied that our reported casualties are absolutely and completely accurate in every degree. In fact, we are reporting rather fuller casualties than we did in the Korean War. Anybody who gets hurt is recorded as wounded, even though he may not be hospitalized.

But as far as the body count on the other side is concerned, I don't know what it is. I wouldn't believe the South Vietnamese figures. I wouldn't believe the figures counted from the gunships as they fly by. I don't know that we know whether bodies counted are soldiers or civilians.

I have disagreed for a long time with the manner in which we use our Air Force, the way we attack villages from the air. I don't know what the actual enemy losses are. But the figures on our casualties, I can assure you, are completely accurate.

Q   What would make President Thieu more amenable to negotiating with the Viet Cong? What specific advice would you give to the President on the problem of President Thieu?

WAH   Insist that Thieu bring into his government representatives of the main body of the people of South Vietnam, the overwhelming majority of whom want peace. We tried through argument to get him to broaden the base of his government, as far back as 1967. So I don't think he will do it himself. If we were to tell Thieu we are going to get all of our troops out in eighteen months—he would be quick to move. Another way is to tell him we will negotiate a separate settlement with the North Vietnamese— without him. Then he probably would do it. But you can't bluff. You have to mean what you say.

He must bring these people in and field a team in Paris that wants to negotiate. Then there would be tough negotiations with the NLF and Hanoi. I am not saying it is going to be easy. But then we would have some chance to come to a settlement which would do what President Johnson and President Nixon both have said they intend—let the South Vietnamese people decide their own future.

But I also would make every effort at once to reduce the level of combat. I would not pay attention to advice which suggests that we are making so much progress that Thieu's military government can win in the long run. We can reduce the level of combat and violence if we go at it right.

Q   Mr. Harriman, you spoke about your views about what President Thieu should do to broaden the base of his government. In view of his past inflexibility, what do you think the chances are that he is willing to take these steps? If not, what measures can our government take?

WAH   Not to be dictated to by him. As I said, we could, if necessary, negotiate in Paris without him. But first, we should insist that he bring into his government representatives of the majority of the people who do want peace. There are a number of ways to do it. The problem is that the policy of the Vietnamization of the war means a continuation of the war. Thieu cannot last if the United States withdrew all its troops. He knows it. We can withdraw some of them—yes, but not all of them if Thieu's government is to last. It was a mistake to take over most of the fighting. But that was changed in 1967 and intensified in 1968 after Tet. It used to be called "de-Americanization." It's not a new policy; it has a new name—"Vietnamization." When General Abrams was appointed deputy to General Westmoreland in the summer of 1967, one of his principal responsibilities was to improve the training of the South Vietnamese armed forces and its officers.

But the problem is that we are going to have to stay there indefinitely if we continue this, although the fighting will be scaled down. If policies giving Thieu a veto are continued, there is no end to this war. The idea that Vietnamization is going to force the North Vietnamese to negotiate on our terms is nonsense. The hope that, if the American people stand behind the Vietnamization plan, Hanoi will give in just doesn't make any sense.

Q   Do you believe there might be a massacre in South Vietnam?

WAH   That has been publicized. Some project it in a good deal of vivid detail. The information that I rely on, which comes back from a number of different sources, including French sources, indicates the other side doesn't want a blood bath. They have said so publicly. I feel sure they would make an agreement for no reprisals with some international supervision to assure it. That should be done. I am not for cut-and-run. There must and there can be an agreement on no reprisals.

I must say that I don't understand what a "just peace" means. Throughout history both sides have gone into war for a "just cause." But as we haven't got a referee, whose "justice" is going to be applied? That doesn't mean anything.

Some people talk about an "honorable" settlement. Are we just trying to save our face and our military honor? No! We have responsibility, and I am for a responsible withdrawal.

Among the things that have to be done is an agreement on no reprisals. And that can be done. Yet, when there is an end of the war, there are going to be problems. There is always going to be some ill-will. With the amount of killing that has been going on in the hamlets and villages there is much bad blood.

Q   Would you comment on the domestic reaction to Mylai?

WAH   I was rather appalled by a poll that indicated public indifference. I don't put much reliance on polls because I believe you can often find what interests you. I see all sorts of polls. I saw a poll the other day on the next President taken by a reputable poll-taker in Delaware in which Ed Muskie ran way ahead of Nixon. Delaware, as you know, was carried by Nixon in 1968. So you can pick the polls.

It's appalling to think that sort of thing can go on. You can't blame only the individuals, as it is the whole system of what we are doing there—the way in which we have permitted indiscriminate dropping of bombs and the shelling in "free fire zones"— dropping them on civilians. If some Viet Cong shot at our aircraft from a hamlet, that was enough to have us bomb and strafe the hamlet, killing a lot of innocent people. Such policies are not the kind that I want to see Americans carry out, and I felt that way some years ago. So I am appalled that people aren't concerned over this, and I don't understand why they aren't concerned. I think everybody

should be very much concerned. We have an obligation now to leave this country of Vietnam in a state
where the people can recover from this destruction.

Now, this idea that we shouldn't take our troops
out because there would be a massacre—people are
now being massacred right and left, all the time. We
have to stop the killing. We have an obligation to
do so. The kind of America that I believe in would
do that.

Q   Sir, you haven't mentioned Laos. What is the logic
of our getting involved there now?

WAH   We were in difficulties in Laos when President
Kennedy came in in 1961. As I have said, Dulles,
Robertson, or someone else reportedly had said in
the late fifties that Laos was to be a "bastion of
Western strength." How you could make Laos into
a "bastion" of anything, I don't know, because the
Laotians are very peace-loving people. In addition,
that attitude was directly provocative to Laos'
neighbors, Red China and North Vietnam. President Kennedy negotiated the Geneva Agreement
of 1962. He was determined not to put in military
forces. He wanted a settlement, and we made, I
think, the best agreement that was possible under
the circumstances.

We made an arrangement under which Souvanna
Phouma headed a neutral coalition government. Unfortunately, the Pathet Lao walked out of that government in 1963 after one of the neutralists had been
killed, stating that it wasn't safe to stay in Vientiane.
The Pathet Lao do not amount to much in the
country at the present time, but the North Vietnam-

ese do. They have maintained routes over the passes into Laos to get down into South Vietnam and Cambodia. And that has been what the major conflict is about. There has been fighting in Laos consistently ever since 1963, and I think the conflict will continue as long as the Vietnamese war continues.

I don't think you can settle Laos until after you settle Vietnam. I am satisfied that we have to make some agreement with Hanoi. They are nationalists and want to be independent of Peking. They are well satisfied with the relations they have established with France, and they want to have normal relations with us, so they can have access to our technology. They want to get miracle rice in order to be independent of China, from whom they now import three hundred thousand tons a year. They want to be independent in other ways, as Tito did. As soon as Tito broke with Stalin he wanted to establish relations with the West. I told the North Vietnamese on a number of occasions that they had to learn to live with their neighbors in peace.

The problem in Laos is that the North Vietnamese have invaded it. This isn't, as some people have said, simply a civil war. This is the North Vietnamese attacking Laos and using it as a corridor to support their actions in South Vietnam. This agreement which we entered into in 1962 was signed by the North Vietnamese too. It was to assure that Laos would be neutral and that it would be left alone by outsiders. It provided that no foreign troops would be introduced into Laos nor would Laos be used as a military base by any of the signatories.

Unfortunately, North Vietnam violated the agreement.

I am not sure that the North Vietnamese want to take over Vientiane. I doubt it. But I think in the Plain of Jars there probably will be shooting for some time to come. It will probably continue until there is a settlement with North Vietnam which leads to a peace in the area. If the countries of Southeast Asia could work together (as President Johnson indicated at Johns Hopkins in 1965) there could be a general program of co-ordinated development in which North Vietnam would participate.

Q   So you take issue with the idea that, in offering a mixed election commission and an election open to all, we have gone as far as we can go, to use Nixon's words?

WAH   I don't understand what was offered. I don't know why the Administration took this rigid position. It never occurred to me that the Communists would enter an election on the basis of the winner taking all. There has to be some prior understanding on other issues. You've got to consider the NLF's ten points.[16] You can't pick just one aspect of settlement. You've got to go through each one of those ten points and see how much you can accept and how much you won't. The Saigon government has its objectives, its eight points; these have to be melded with those of the NLF.

I don't think it's a reasonable proposition to just

[16] The National Liberation Front put forward in Paris May 1969 a ten-point proposal that outlined its negotiating position. This was elaborated on by an eight-point statement in September 1970.

pick one point, an election, particularly as the government continues to put people in jail for political reasons. They give no real assurance so far that there would be completely free discussion or free campaigning for NLF candidates.

So you have to have some prior understandings. For instance, you would want to be sure that there would be no reprisals against anyone for their past political actions. If there is to be a political settlement, it must provide for the personal safety of people on both sides. Of course, of first importance is the exchange of prisoners of war and then amnesty for all in jail or in exile for political reasons. In addition, there might be an understanding about postponing reunification. My own feeling has been that the NLF has been rather keen to see South Vietnam independent of the North for some years. They probably want to delay reunification until the South is as strong as the North. I have thought they'd agree to postponing any merger for a period of five to ten years. But they would want at once normalization of relations between the North and South with free movement of people and goods.

Another point that could be discussed is the character of the postwar society in the South. The NLF's 1967 program included a provision that the social-economic structure would seem to be a mixed socialist and capitalist society. Peasants would own their own farms. Private capital, both domestic and foreign, would be encouraged in some activities. These are things which might be talked out, and if you could get an arrangement which had some lasting qualities about it, then there'd be a chance for it to succeed.[17]

I have selected this question from the New York *Times Magazine* interview of August 1969 because, taken together with the answer to the previous question, it gives an outline of the kind of settlement I believed then—and still believe— might be worked out through negotiations among the Vietnamese themselves. This requires the Saigon government to reverse its stand against any compromise settlement. The United States would have to give assurance of the total withdrawal of all U.S. forces and agree that South Vietnam would become neutral and non-aligned. As I indicated in answering the prior question, of parallel importance is an agreement between Washington and Hanoi for cooperation in reconstruction and development in the area, which is in Hanoi's interest to keep and, of course, for strict adherence to the 1962 Laos agreement.

[17] This question and answer drawn with minor clarifications from "Harriman Suggests a Way Out of Vietnam," by Hedrick Smith, New York *Times Magazine*, August 24, 1969. Used with permission.

FUTURE

I DON'T LIKE THE CONCLUSION OF anything, but it is not the end that I am going to consider. I am now going to discuss the future. I have often been asked by the press what's going to happen, and I have come to have a regular answer, "I am not hired to be a prophet." It is particularly dangerous to prophesy about the Soviet Union.

Yet there are some fundamentals about Russia and America which we should bear in mind and some policies and attitudes we should adopt. First of all, we must recognize that what we do here in the United States will have an influence on Soviet attitudes and actions. So, I am going to say something about ourselves first.

Somehow or other we have gotten off the path that I thought we should have continued to follow. People the world over were inspired by President Roosevelt. He had the faculty of talking to people over the heads of governments, convincing them of his sincere interest in them and of his determination to seek a peaceful world. In his Good Neighbor Policy he could do little at the time but he convinced the Latin Americans that we had abandoned intervention, abandoned landing the Marines, and that we were going to be good neighbors, take an interest and be concerned about their problems. In the Soviet Union as well as in Latin America, his name is still alive. People still speak of him as a man who would have led us toward peace—things would have been different had he lived. When he died, the Soviet people had lost a friend. Women wept in the streets, men were deeply disturbed, and even Stalin, when I went to see him, showed grave concern.

I remember his toast to Roosevelt at a dinner Stalin gave De Gaulle during the war. He didn't like De Gaulle very much. De Gaulle had been rather stiff. I sat next to Stalin, and he turned to me and said, "General de Gaulle, he is an awkward and stubborn man." However, I was strongly for De Gaulle that night as he was standing firm against Stalin on principles important to us at the time. He had stoutly refused to recognize the Communist-controlled Lublin Poles as the legitimate Polish government, a precondition Stalin was demanding for a defense treaty De Gaulle was much interested in obtaining.

Stalin finally gave in later that night. But at dinner Stalin wanted to show De Gaulle that he thought very little of him and of France and a great deal of his American and British allies. He spoke about Roosevelt and Churchill. He gave toasts to the achievements of the Allies. In his toast to Churchill he called him "my friend and collaborator in this war, a man of indestructible fighting spirit." I was struck by the phrase "in this war." On the other hand his toast to Roosevelt was, "a great leader for peace as well as for war."

Roosevelt's name is still remembered in Russia with reverence because he symbolizes the hope for peace and the friendship between our two countries the people crave. And the same is true for John F. Kennedy in many parts of the world. I was surprised how quickly he got over the blunder of the Bay of Pigs and how much his words and actions appealed to people. Again, they felt he cared about them—and they were right. In Latin America his name is revered—peasants keep his picture on the walls of their small huts.

These men spoke for the kind of America that means much to me, America that is interested in other people. We have our own interests, yes. And in international affairs one has to look after the interests of one's country. But there has always been an America—one that I knew and profoundly respected, which was concerned about other people, willing to be a good neighbor, willing to hold out a hand in friendship.

I was surprised that President Nixon announced as a new policy "self-help" in economic development. President Truman's policy in the Marshall Plan was to encourage the Europeans for "self-help and mutual aid." That was the whole conception, and we emphasized it in everything we said and did. The entire gross national product of the sixteen countries engaged in the Marshall Plan in Europe was only about one hundred billion dollars at that time. (It is now nearly four times that in constant dollars.) We were giving something over five billion for the first year so we publicized that Europeans were doing 95 per cent of the job, whereas we were doing only 5 per cent. In fact, we made the Europeans undertake responsibilities which they did not want. We insisted that they divide the aid, so that it would be their decision on which country got how much. Some of us felt that if we Americans made the division, we would be blamed by everybody because none would think they got their fair share. We wanted the Europeans to be independent and to cooperate together more closely. This worked remarkably well. We have every right to be proud of what our country did at that time.

President Truman took extraordinary initiatives and gained the enormous respect of people everywhere. In Turkey and Greece particularly his name is one that is always remembered because he came to their help in their hour of need. The Marshall Plan, of course, gave encouragement to Western Europe, but the Point Four proposal, when President Truman announced it in 1949, was hailed world-wide among the impoverished peoples. It gave new hope.

Something changed with Dulles—his talk about the immorality of neutrality, and "brinkmanship," and his other insensitive attitudes. If this comment appears to be partisan, I want to add that President Eisenhower, too, had the good will of people around the world. There was great respect and affection for him personally. But Dulles offended people by asserting that those who were neutral were immoral because they hadn't made the issue between right and wrong. Communism was evil, and therefore we were always right. It took us a long time to get over the labeling of neutrals as immoral. I am not sure we have fully gotten over it yet.

We should respect neutrality. We have to respect neutrality. For a large part of our life as a nation we were neutral, and how in the world we could condemn neutrality is something I couldn't understand at the time, and can't now. President Kennedy, however, returned to our earlier conceptions. He spoke of a "world safe for diversity" and worked for the neutrality of Laos. He helped enormously to re-establish the good will that we had previously had in the world.

Now, there are other things which have set us back. Vietnam came. I want to say that one of the things President Nixon has stated—that we have to stay in Vietnam in order to avoid "a collapse in confidence in American leadership"—just isn't true. I know it not to be true. During President Johnson's Administration, between the years of 1964 and 1968, I went to fifty countries and a number of them several times. They were fairly evenly divided between Latin America, Europe, Africa, the Middle East, and the Far East. I talked to heads of governments in almost every case. I saw the local press, I talked to our American correspondents (whose knowledge and "feel" I have learned to respect over the years). Of course, I talked with the people in our Embassies. Except in the Far East, I can say it was difficult to find people who would support our position in Vietnam, and even in Asia there are questions raised about it.

In Europe one head of government publicly supported our position, and that was Harold Wilson, the British Prime Minister. He did that at considerable sacrifice to his position in his own party. Of course Britain needed our help because of the difficulties the pound was in at that time.

In Africa another was the capable and friendly President of Tunisia, Habib Bourguiba who has been strongly for our policy in Vietnam. He had a definite reason. His is a small country worried about its neighbors, Algeria on one side and Nasser just a bit away on the other. He is now perhaps also somewhat concerned by the military government friendly to Nasser that has taken over his neighbor, Libya. He sees the Sixth Fleet steaming up and down the Mediterranean and would like to have it come to his assistance if he should get into trouble. But you have to look quite far to find people that will support us.

I can say with confidence that the world generally would be extremely happy if we find a way to end this war in Vietnam. People do not understand why we are there; they are not convinced as to the motivations; they are horrified by many of the things they hear are going on there; and there would be great relief if we found a way to end this war.

Then I think we could rebuild the position in the world we have lost, in no small part due to Vietnam.

So, the re-establishment of our moral leadership in the world is, I think, one of the most important things for us to do. I think it will have an important influence on our relations with the Soviet Union. Our strength is not military strength alone, but also the position and influence we have in the world which impresses people. You can call it prestige if you want; I would much prefer to speak of it as moral leadership. It's respect for us.

In the Marshall Plan days I used to have arguments in the congressional committees before whom I appeared when we were attempting to get those enormous appropriations. One time several congressmen were pressing me for indications that the Europeans were grateful. I told them that I thought gratitude was the last emotion that we wanted to evoke. In the first place, it's an emotion that doesn't last for long. It's the old story of the way to make an enemy is to lend a man some money. What we tried to do was to build respect and confidence. The congressmen pressed me rather hard, and I grew rather annoyed. Finally, I said something along these lines: "I know exactly what you would like me to do. You would like to have me bring pictures of children dancing in the squares of the provincial towns of France, waving American flags and singing 'God Bless America.'" I said, "That's exactly what I am *not* going to do. You can fire me if you want, but as long as I am here, that's exactly what we are not going to encourage. If it happens spontaneously, occasionally, why that is something else." We were trying to cultivate initiative and independence—not gratitude or dependence. We were, in fact, gaining respect and confidence in our purpose.

If we are to be effective leaders in the world, we have to understand the kind of attitude we must assume. We didn't seek leadership in the world. It was thrust upon us. However, the responsibility of leadership is now real. The world is not as good a place if we fail to exercise it wisely and responsibly. Furthermore what we do now and how we develop our attitude toward world problems will have an effect on Soviet behavior.

I had a chance to see even in my first wartime visit to Moscow in September 1941 that our attitude did affect the influence of personalities, sometimes for better and sometimes for worse. During one of Beaverbrook's and my talks with Stalin the subject of our respective Ambassadors came up. Stalin was quite blunt in expressing his views, and this made it possible for me also to be direct. Oumanski was the Soviet Ambassador in Washington at the time, and I knew he was not too well regarded by our people who had to deal with him. He was considered to be uncooperative, rigid and carrying on questionable propaganda. So when Stalin asked me about him, I told Stalin my impression was that he was overzealous in watching out for Soviet interests in the United States. I said I thought Soviet interests would be best served by a man who knew us and how to get along with us. As a result Oumanski was transferred to Mexico and replaced by Litvinov in Washington. His presence as Soviet wartime Ambassador certainly helped our mutual relations during that critical period.

When I reported to President Roosevelt on my return, I told him about how difficult Molotov was to deal with and that I did not believe we could improve our relations with the Soviets as long as he was Foreign Minister. I explained that if one could get past Molotov to Stalin, it was easier to get a favorable response from Stalin. I thought from the way Molotov behaved in Stalin's presence and the way Stalin treated him that Molotov was still in the dog house and had not been forgiven for the failure of the Ribbentrop Treaty. I therefore recommended to President Roosevelt that he pay no attention to Molotov and make it obvious he was not willing to deal with him. However, neither President Roosevelt nor Harry Hopkins took what I said seriously. Molotov was invited to Washington in the spring of 1942 and shown marked courtesies. From Washington he proceeded to London where he signed a treaty of alliance and mutual assistance with the British, the principles of which Eden had negotiated with Stalin some months earlier. I met him again in Moscow when I was there with Churchill in August 1942. The change in his attitude from my previous visit was apparent. He was swollen up like a poison toad. Instead of being in Stalin's bad graces he was self-assured and aggressive.

Whether a different attitude on our part would have led to minimizing Molotov's influence or even to his transfer from the foreign ministry, is impossible to say, but I feel we did help to rehabilitate him with Stalin, and he played an increasingly important and unhelpful role. "Nyet" was the word he liked the most, and his influence continued to be negative. I was confirmed in my opinion when Khrushchev told me in 1959 if he had listened to Molotov there would have been no Trieste compromise nor the important Austrian State Treaty.

I have also spoken of the fact that the Soviets were changing life within their own country itself. There is an odd word that has been used by some people, including some in Russia —"convergence." The idea is that the problems of modern life—rational economic organization, scientific development, control and use of nuclear energy, mass production, education, health, city planning, protection of the environment and the like—are substantially the same for both countries, and that as we deal with them we will grow very much alike. I cannot accept fully the theory of convergence, although I do believe that some of our differences will be reduced. President Roosevelt thought if we could work together with the Soviets during the immediate postwar years a number of our differences would smooth out. They would move toward our freedoms, and our government would undertake an increasing role in our social and economic life. I agreed with President Roosevelt in principle but I wasn't as optimistic as Roosevelt about the pace at which changes within the Soviet Union would occur.

I utterly disagree with those who contend the difference now between the two of us is just our economic systems. That aspect is relatively unimportant. Nations are not going to fight over economic theories. Our "free enterprise system" is different than it used to be. The vastly increasing size of corporations and institutions has created new and unsolved problems.

Professor Galbraith suggests that "Convergence begins with modern large-scale production . . . ," and he notes that "nothing . . . is more interesting than that the erstwhile capitalist corporation and the erstwhile Communist firm should, under the imperatives of organization, come together as oligarchies of their own members. Ideology is not the relevant force."

Ken points things out at times in a way to shock some people and to jar them out of their complacency. He has originated and popularized sound economic concepts that were first scorned and are now generally accepted. Who would have thought that the "minimum family income," though not his specific suggestion, would now be proposed by a Republican administration?[1]

Our social and economic system is working perhaps toward Swedish socialist concepts but not toward Soviet

[1] On foreign policy, Galbraith was already warning President Kennedy as early as 1961 and 1962 not to get more deeply involved in support of Diem's regime, nor to engage American troops in Vietnam. No one has a better right now to lead in the battle for peace in Vietnam.

Communism. The government in Sweden has overcome poverty, achieved decent housing and medical service for all, but Sweden has in no way compromised the principle of representative government and concern for civil liberties.

A basic difference between the Soviet Union and us is our fundamental idea that government is here to be the servant of the people and not the reverse. That is a very fundamental difference and we certainly are not going to weaken our principles of representative government and civil liberties. It is going to take a long time to get Soviet convergence on that.

Individual initiative is a vital force in our society. There is something pretty good about our system when you get a young man like Ralph Nader—a man who has the courage, the knowledge, the facts, to defy one of the largest corporations in our country and force changes in design. That's a rather extraordinary achievement, although it's certainly not his only nor his most important one. He has aroused our country to think quite differently about a great many subjects. He has had enormous influence. Naturally, I don't agree with everything he and his "raiders" have said. Sometimes they are a bit too superficial and self-assured in their analysis. But basically he is on the right track, and it is an extraordinary thing that a young man of that type with high ideals can have the influence he has, and it gives me great heart that the individual still counts the most in our country. No matter how big our institutions become, we are as strong as our individuals are, not as strong as the state is.

Therefore I am not unduly disturbed by this generation of students. I don't condone in any way the extremes that have led to violence at some universities. I don't agree at all with things some do, but by and large, I think this generation of students has the chance to become the most constructive in my lifetime. Why? Because they are concerned about what is going on in our country. The thoughtful are ready to take responsibility for it. That is why I encourage students to get on with their participation in the political life of our country. These days people call it "working within the system."

I agree with the idea, but I don't particularly like the phrase. The word "system" implies something rigid, unchanging. Communism is a "system." Fascism is a "system." But ours isn't a rigid society. Ours is a society of infinite flexibilities. That flexibility is what has kept it alive and resilient, capable of change and innovation.

We should remember that the American flag was the flag of our Revolution. It was not the flag of the stand-patters. We cannot now let demagogues, or chauvinists, or misguided hard-hats take patriotism and the American flag as their exclusive banner. To me the true patriots are those dedicated to our principles of justice and equality to all here at home and to restoring us to our place in the world as an understanding and responsible Good Neighbor and the leading standard-bearer of peace.

I am heartened by the work the students have been doing in Washington in lobbying against the war and in the manner in which they are organizing to participate in this year's elections. Their example stimulated a thousand Wall Street lawyers, some of them from the most conservative firms, to go to Washington and, from the steps of the Capitol, urge the Congress to take action to stop the war.[2]

[2] Extracted from Address at Twenty-fifth Anniversary Memorial Ceremony for Franklin D. Roosevelt, May 30, 1970, and Commencement Address at Georgetown University, June 7, 1970.

Students can play a very important role. If I knew what they will do with this country, what their generation will do, I perhaps could tell you a little more about what will happen with Russia.

One vital question is our military position. It is appalling to me that there is so much emphasis today on arms. The Administration's meaning of nuclear "sufficiency" has not been clearly defined. It is essential to maintain a deterrent but how much "overkill" do we need? I have known many of the scientific advisers of Eisenhower, Kennedy, and Johnson. I know pretty much what they think. It is quite different from the scientific position that the Pentagon is taking. These men don't want to embark on new weapons systems at the moment we are negotiating with the Russians for restraint. Unfortunately, competition between our military services contributes to the demand for new weapons.

I have been working much of my life to get adequate military preparedness—both before Pearl Harbor and after the war. Now we have it; now I find myself believing that the most important thing to do is to reduce the military budget. We must get it under control. More important than more weapons is our influence in the world. We have a compelling job to do in our country—to make our society one which gives an opportunity for all and to catch up with the abuse of our environment. These are very real needs and are absolutely essential.

In the present world situation we have to keep a sufficiently strong military position, but we have to guard against a growing arrogance of power. I don't like to admit it, but the danger exists. As Senator J. William Fulbright, the Chairman of the Senate Foreign Relations Committee, has written, "Gradually but unmistakably America is showing signs of that arrogance of power which has afflicted, weakened, and in some cases destroyed great nations in the past. In so doing we are not living up to our capacity and promise as a civilized example for the world."

Small-minded people cloak themselves in American power and become arrogant. They talk about dropping bombs and forcing our will on others. These are things that appall me, and the influence in our political life of people with such attitudes has to be resisted.

It is significant that it took eight years before President Eisenhower's remark about the dangers of the industrial-military complex began to be understood. I wrote an article for *Look*, in which I pointed out that the military-congressional complex was the one that concerned me more. I am disturbed that some armed services committee members and others in both the House and the Senate have been involved for so long a time with military matters that they have come to feel armaments are the most important thing. They are the ones that are peddling the wares of the military. In fact, until 1969 the Congress often voted more money for defense than the Secretary of Defense asked for.

I quote from my *Look* article of August 1969:

Like many other Americans, I am fearful about the present role of the military in our national life. Military men have as their primary responsibility the defense of the nation, and they are miscast when they are expected to be omniscient on other vital national concerns. It is in some ways unfair to ask them to accept responsibility for decisions on which they are clearly unqualified to give a balanced judgment.

I have worked closely with our military officers during the past three decades and respect them for their competence and dedication to our country. I have held many of them in the highest esteem, among them General Marshall. I vividly recall Marshall explaining to President Roosevelt that his advice was given purely from a military standpoint. [General Omar Bradley was a stout, wise, and courageous adviser to President Truman in the critical days of the Korean War. General John R. Deane, head of our wartime military mission in Moscow, together with his colleagues, worked as an integral part of our Embassy team. His resourcefulness and insight contributed greatly to our effectiveness.][3]

In 1941, I was in London as President Roosevelt's personal representative to Prime Minister Churchill and the British Government. Even then, I was struck by the difference in the role of the military in Britain and in the U.S. The British War Cabinet consisted of the political leaders of the country, and the ministers of the armed services were not even members of it. I am not suggesting that the British military leaders were not highly respected or that their views were not given full weight. But they were given weight within the Cabinet in balance with the other problems of the British nation. The military chiefs of staff were advisers to the Cabinet. The military establishment was integrated into the policy-making procedures of the British government. They had no contact with the Parliament, nor did they give any public expression of their views.

This is altogether different from our present procedures. Not only the Secretary of Defense but also

[3] General Deane's book, *The Strange Alliance*, published in 1946 gives a vivid account of our wartime relations with the Russians.

the Chiefs of Staff go to the committees of the Congress and testify on all sorts of matters. As a result, a number of senators and congressmen get an unbalanced view of our nation's needs from military men who are responsible for only one aspect of our national concerns. What I am suggesting is that we have a group of senators and congressmen whose attention is concentrated on military needs. That is why we had one member of the Congress saying a short while back that if we turned over the Vietnam war to the soldiers, they would win it in a month.

Nothing could be more absurd than that statement. But it indicates the mind-set that some members of Congress get after steady bombardment by the views of our military. Their responsibility is the security of the nation, and they must look at the worst of everything. Those who see only the possible military threats would drive us into another world war. That is why isolated military judgments of political situations are not sound. Robert Kennedy wrote that during the Cuban missile crisis, he was struck by how often his brother's military advisers took "positions, which, if wrong, had the advantage that no one would be around at the end to know" how wrong they were. . . .

It is reassuring that the Congress is increasingly showing concern over military programs and exercising its independent judgments on decisions.

I believe that negotiations we are now starting with the Soviets to control the nuclear arms race are the most important we have ever undertaken. They can be successful if we act wisely. From my talks with Mr. Kosygin and other Soviet officials, I

am satisfied that they want to stop the nuclear arms
race. . . .[4]

I am highly gratified that so many senators stood up last
year against the ABM. They lost by only one vote. I hope
that there will be a real fight against the new ABM proposal
and that this year it will be won.[5]

We would have a much better chance to get a better settlement in the SALT talks if we showed restraint. It is folly to
think that we have to go ahead spending billions for ABMs
to add cards to our hand for negotiations. It discredits us and
only strengthens the influence of the more suspicious hard-
liners in Moscow, and has apparently encouraged similar
escalation on the part of the Soviet Union. I have explained the
way President Kennedy got talks going on the test ban by
announcing that he was going to stop the testing in the
atmosphere, providing the other side did so also. With a
promise of similar restraint on the Soviet side President Nixon
should have announced early in 1969 that we would hold up
testing and deployment of MIRVs and ABMs. We can afford
to wait. We are not stripped of deterrents. Look at the figures.
Even if our Minuteman missiles are getting obsolescent because they are too vulnerable as some scientists have said,
we still have our submarine force, as well as our bomber force.
The submarines are untouchable, and there is no danger to
them in the foreseeable future—at least those that are at sea.
There is adequate power there alone to deter any reckless
actions.

Recent events tend to confirm the fear that the opportunity which existed in the first half of 1969 to get a much more

[4] Extract from "Our Security Lies Beyond Weapons," *Look*, August 26,
1969. Copyright © 1969, Cowles Communications, Inc. Used with permission.

[5] An amendment to limit the Administration's proposal for additional
ABM deployment was defeated in the Senate, 52–47, in August 1970.

comprehensive agreement has been tragically missed by the failure of either side to propose the exercise of mutual restraint. Because of continued developments by both countries any agreement coming out of the current talks can apparently be only limited in scope.

Furthermore, this idea that we are going to get along better with China by spending tens of billions of dollars on a thin ABM defense against her doesn't make any sense. If our deterrent is adequate to prevent an attack by Russia with its vast nuclear capability, why shouldn't it be adequate against China that for decades will have only limited capability?

These are problems the coming generation is going to be faced with; it is going to have its part in the world—in how that world is shaped. I say today it is no longer a question of guns and butter; it is a question of bigger guns against the health of our national life. We have to recognize that and stop the overspending on bigger guns.

There are many casualties of Vietnam other than the men that have been lost there. One is our aid program to developing nations.

It is natural and right for people to want to avoid future involvements in situations like Vietnam. But it is nonsense to argue that aid programs as such will get us into new Vietnams.

At the very time President Truman was undertaking extraordinary aid programs in Western Europe and through Point Four, he understood there were limits to our capabilities. For example, he recognized that in China there was nothing feasible we could do, and in spite of criticism he refrained from becoming involved in the civil war there. The fact that we had been giving large amounts of economic and military assistance to Chiang Kai-shek's Nationalist government did not affect his decision.

The important thing to learn from Vietnam is not to take political responsibility for specific governments and not to involve American forces in their defense. Of course aid given through multilateral institutions or programs has the advantage of limiting direct political involvement.

But our responsibilities in the world to help the under-developed countries are very real. I commend to you the report of Mike Pearson, the Canadian statesman and chairman of the United Nations Commission on International Development.[6] It brings out clearly the fact that the capital that is being made available to the less developed countries is utterly inadequate. We used to carry the major load. But the Pearson report shows that the United States is lagging behind industrial countries and in 1968, ranked eighth in terms of the percentage of our gross national product devoted to assistance. Since then we have fallen even lower—to eleventh place. We all agree that multilateralization of development assistance so far as it can be done, is desirable. This can be done through international agencies and through consortia or groups for special purposes and individual countries. Then there is the staggering problem of population growth and the need to expand food production.

But fundamentally we have to give a helping hand. It isn't a question of whether we want to. It is utterly impossible to think we can live happily in great wealth with poverty all around us. Western Europe and Japan are doing well, but about half the population of the non-Communist world has an annual per-capita income of something like one hundred dol-

[6] Lester B. Pearson, formerly Prime Minister of Canada and President of the United Nations General Assembly.

lars. Remember that we in the United States are talking about thirty-seven hundred dollars as a minimum for a family of four. Anything below that is regarded as poverty level.

It's popular to sneer at what has been done, and there has been wide publicity about some of the failures. We should learn from these mistakes and not be scared off by them. Any objective study will show that over the years there have been many very great achievements. Of course, our programs in Western Europe, Germany, and Japan were a fantastic success. However, progress in the underdeveloped countries hasn't been as rapid as we had hoped for. There are certain countries like Korea and Taiwan that have done remarkably well, others have been rather slow. Some Latin American countries have made real progress, whereas others have been disappointing partly because social reforms have been so slow in the making and partly because of the effect of rapid population growth. But we cannot force social reforms on others. Unfortunately, it is very difficult to put political conditions on our help, except the condition that for a specific project it is used well.

I recently testified before a subcommittee of the Joint Economic Committee of the Congress as follows:

> In September 1969 President Nixon appointed a Presidential Task Force on International Development with Rudolph A. Peterson as Chairman.[7] I strongly endorse the basic findings of this group, particularly the principle of multilateralism—that our program should be carried forward through international institutions or in cooperation with other countries. . . .
> One of the difficulties of developing nations is

[7] President of the Bank of America.

that debt service is growing and absorbing a larger and larger percentage of their exports. This burden has nearly doubled during the past decade. . . . We should be prepared to cooperate with other industrial countries in renegotiation of debt service where the burden is too great. . . .

In helping economic development, aid is only one facet. International efforts should be directed toward assisting and encouraging the exports of the developing nations. Of prime importance is co-operation among the importing countries for greater stability in price and volume of primary products. Feast or famine in these exports cause serious economic dislocations in the supplying countries— either disastrous inflation or depression. Surely it is in the interest of both supplier and user to seek more stabilized markets in these products. A start has been made, but more progress is needed.

In addition, to achieve sound economies with more jobs and growth, the developing countries must expand their exports of manufactured products. It is essential that they have access to expanding markets in the industrialized states.

These imports may cause some dislocation in our own industrial production. Wherever this occurs, our government should give assistance. Not only should the displaced workers be assisted by re-training, but the companies involved should be encouraged and assisted in developing new products and the communities stimulated to attract new industries.

We should bear in mind that the industries affected usually are low-wage industries, and the net effect can well lead to the expansion of our higher pay industries. We have seen this sort of thing develop in New York State where low-wage textile industries have gone to the South. Communities that had initiative have attracted new industries with higher wage rates and thereby have prospered. The same principle is applicable in connection with our trade policies.

Another vital element along with trade and aid is private investment, both domestic and foreign. The Congress has recently enacted legislation creating the Overseas Private Investment Corporation (OPIC) to provide a new means of protecting the American investor against political risks. Of course, to be successful, U.S. investors must have an understanding of local attitudes and consideration of national interest in connection with their undertakings. Foreign investors should give more consideration to manufacturing and distributing activities rather than concentrating, as has been the case in the past, in mining and other extractive industries. Since the days when the *conquistadors* stripped the Aztecs of their gold, foreign mining has been regarded as exploitation south of the Rio Grande.

[A success story of American investment in Latin America has been the experience of Sears Roebuck. I have followed with interest their operations since they started in Mexico in 1947.

In the beginning they had to import from the United States almost all of what they sold, but gradually they have encouraged Mexican production so that now I understand that 99% of their sales are manufactured in Mexico. It is small wonder that their operations have been recognized as a boon to the country. They have brought not only sound merchandising methods which have reduced the cost to the consumer, but have helped build industry and employment. They have given technical assistance and helped start and finance the local enterprises. As soon as possible, they have substituted Mexicans for American members of their staff. In addition, they have applied their employee profit-sharing plan to their Mexican employees.

Sears Roebuck has in the same manner expanded its operations to Venezuela, Colombia, Brazil, Peru, and all but one of the Central American countries; and except for Cuba there has been little local anti-American agitation against them.

I think Sears Roebuck—although of course not the only one—is an outstanding example of American initiative in understanding and contributing to the welfare of our Latin American neighbors.]

I completed my testimony before the subcommittee as follows:

In conclusion, there are important reasons why we must continue our concern for and our assistance to the developing nations. First of all is our moral obligation. We have been endowed with resources which have made it possible for us to achieve a prosperity unheard of in history, and surely we have an obligation to give a helping hand to the less fortunate.

Secondly, our own economic life can be strengthened and expanded as other nations develop. Expanding trade and markets will add greatly to our own continuing prosperity.

Lastly, the very survival of our civilization is at stake. The Pearson Report points out that 34% of the population of the world in the developed nations has 87½% of the world's gross national product, whereas the 66% in the less developed nations have only 12½%. It is not conceivable that a few countries can live indefinitely as islands of luxury in a sea of poverty.[8]

I hope the President will in accordance with his assurances submit a new aid program and will give it the vigorous support necessary to get it through the Congress. Without strong presidential backing it is difficult to get members of the Congress to vote for foreign aid since recipients of foreign aid do not vote in this country. A congressman can only justify his vote if the President emphasizes to the Congress that the nation's welfare is involved. He cannot be expected to convince his constituents by his own argument alone. Aid appropriations have fallen to a new low because the President has not been willing to put up a fight.

On the other hand I do commend the President for other important actions that he has taken such as those relating to bacteriological and chemical warfare.

We ought to understand where the Russians are dangerous and where they are not. There used to be an idea that any time a developing country took aid from the Soviets, it would get scarlet fever. I have found that isn't true at all. For example, the Soviets have given aid in long-term credits to India for some time, and it has been useful. In 1959 I went to the Belai steel works, which the Russians had contracted

[8] Extract from Testimony before the Subcommittee on Foreign Economic Policy of the Joint Economic Committee of the Congress May 14, 1970.

to build, and I was quite surprised at the way in which it was being carried out. They were training the Indians to do the job. We have a habit (and so do the Europeans) of what is called "turn key"—build the plant and hand over the key. But the Soviets were training the Indian engineers during the construction period to take over their operating responsibilities. The Russians had evidently developed this method in their aid program in China.

I talked to the chief Russian engineer, whom I had met during the war. He described their procedures, and they appeared to be working well. In their contract the Soviets had agreed to keep a few experts there for three or four years after the construction was finished. This led to the suspicion that they wanted to keep control of the operation for subversive reasons. They did have quite an active secret police, but I gathered its activities were to see that their own Russian staff was not subverted by the Indians. The Russians had to go to weekly indoctrination lectures and movies that bored them to death. They were restricted in their contacts with Indians. For instance, I was told that one of them was not even allowed to go fishing alone with his opposite number on the Indian staff. It is true however, that the Communists were trying to infiltrate the unions, but it was being done largely through Soviet-trained Indian nationals. As far as the Russian staff working on the steel mill was concerned, the Soviets wanted to make sure their own men would not be subverted. This is the sort of thing that we ought to understand, and we ought to have sense enough to welcome Russian assistance to countries like India when they are engaged in constructive projects.

In Black Africa the Soviets have had very limited success in penetration. The new African countries are highly nationalistic.

In many cases they have been disillusioned because Russian equipment is often not good for the tropics, and in other ways the Soviets have had rather unrewarding results. The young Africans who have gone to the Soviet Union to study have run into racial hostility, and most of them have returned home disenchanted. The president of one of the French-speaking African countries told me with a smile, "If you want to produce a Communist send a student to Paris. If you want him to be anti-Communist send him to Russia."

As for the Red Chinese, most Africans are wary of them. They know of the population pressures in China, and they fear an attempt by the Chinese to colonize the underpopulated parts of Africa. This does not mean that they do not welcome Red China's contribution to the Tanzam railroad from Dar es Salaam to Zambia.

The British and the United States advised against this highly popular project as being too costly and uneconomic. Peking, however, is now financing and helping to build it with a loan of some four hundred million dollars repayable over thirty years *without interest*. The impact of this undertaking and the exemplary behavior so far of the Chinese on the job may have a far-reaching effect on Red China's future influence in Africa.

European countries—particularly France—are making substantial contributions to the development of the African countries which had formerly been their colonies. It is to our own long-range interest to contribute as well and to encourage other industrial nations to do the same. The Chinese Nationalists have done very effective work in giving technical assistance, such as in growing rice. They send families to show how the work is done. To see the Chinese men working alongside their wives in the fields is a useful example to the Africans who have customarily left such work to their women.

Israel has also been most helpful in development of useful industrial and other projects.

I think President Nixon is quite right when he says Japan is ready to take on more responsibility. In fact Japan has been increasingly assuming more responsibility during the past decade. For example in the new Asian Development Bank, Japan's contribution is equal to our own. How far it is wise now for us to encourage the Japanese to arm themselves should be examined with great care. We did encourage Germany to rearm, but within NATO and I think it has been effective and absolutely essential.

I want to repeat in a little more detail the fact that the Russians have a number of different ways of operating abroad. Like Stalin, the present group is motivated by Russian imperialism. We find them trying to achieve similar objectives to those of czarist Russia.

The Russians have historically felt bottled up in the Black Sea and have wanted free access in the Mediterranean with an assured outlet to the Atlantic and through the Suez Canal to the Indian Ocean. As I mentioned, Stalin told me of the importance he placed on a navy and a merchant marine. I have not been surprised by the naval construction the Soviet Union has undertaken and the appearance of the Russian navy in the Mediterranean. We cannot deny the Soviet Union peaceful use of the Mediterranean and unfortunately that includes naval presence. We have to take this in our stride. We have no basis for considering the Mediterranean a *mare Americana*, although we should support Europe's vital interest to prevent its becoming Russian-dominated.

Moreover, the Czars always wanted to expand their influence in the Middle East. In recent years this area has become increasingly important with its vast oil resources. Although we get only a relatively small amount of our oil consumption from North Africa and the Middle East, the area currently supplies some 80 per cent of Western Europe's requirements. The Arab-Israeli confrontation has now given the Soviets a means of vastly increasing their influence throughout the region, particularly with the radical Arab leaders. It is significant that the Soviet government has supported these radicals even though they are non-Communist and even put the leaders of the local Communists in jail. This has been true of Nasser in the UAR and elsewhere—recently in Syria. The Soviet leaders possibly think that in time they can replace the present radicals with Communists, but they are biding their time and dealing with the present leaders regardless of the effect on the local Communist parties.

I am satisfied that the Soviet Union, however, does not wish to let the conflict between the Arabs and Israeli develop to the point of war between the United States and the Soviet Union. But it is hard to know how much "brinkmanship" they will indulge in. The two-handed policy the State Department has consistently recommended will not be adequate to quiet the Arabs' resentment of our supplying arms to Israel, which we must do. Then, too, the influence of the Palestinian guerrillas has vastly increased in the last three years. They are far more militant than the leaders of the Arab nations. They are already dominating the Jordanian scene and have forced Lebanon to change its former policy of neutrality. They are insisting on no settlement with Israel. Although they are not a government and are divided among themselves, some way must be found to deal directly with them if peace is to be attained.

It is now hard to see how this unhappy situation can be

brought to a peaceful solution. We must continue to press the Soviet Union to use its influence for a settlement. Without Soviet arms, the Arabs would be helpless. We must also see that Israel is adequately supplied with arms, to assure its defense. We should do what we can to mobilize world opinion against Soviet aggressive military support of Egypt, including the further introduction of Soviet airmen and anti-aircraft gunners. Our influence in the Middle East and in the world would be vastly increased if we could end the war in Indo-China. Our position as a force for peace has been clouded by world-wide misgivings about what we are doing there.

I still believe that with persistence and firmness we can bring the Russians to a more responsible position and eventually bring about a settlement. The Soviets don't want war with us and they don't like the diversion of resources from their domestic requirements that is necessary to arm the Arabs. At some stage they may feel that the favorable results of their present policies have reached the point of diminishing return and will be ready to join in a peaceful settlement. We should never give up.[9]

In other parts of the world, the historic conflict between Russia and China is, I believe, being fanned by the ideological differences between Moscow and Peking. The Soviet Union will be attempting to offset Red China's influence in the Far East. The Japanese government in the immediate postwar period was more concerned over difficulties with the Soviet Union than with Red China. Historically, Russia had been Japan's enemy, whereas the Japanese have never feared China because of their superior organization and industrialization. Things seem to be changing now and I believe that Russia and

[9] Written before the American initiative for a cease-fire, with the subsequent violations, and the death of President Nasser, but these general observations still apply.

Japan will find more common ground in the future. Japan will become increasingly concerned over Red China.

In Indonesia, the Russians attempted with large economic and military credits, to increase their influence with Sukarno at the expense of Peking and the West. This failed. Now the Soviet Union is ready to adopt parallel policies with the Western creditors in deferring repayment of loans (of which they hold half) and in giving additional credits to the new government.

Parallel policies have also developed in the Subcontinent—India and Pakistan—and I believe, as I have indicated, that similar policies can develop in Southeast Asia. If we can come to further understanding with the Soviet over control of nuclear weapons, we will be in a better position to consult together over the future threat of China's nuclear developments.

In Europe we have a new situation with Willy Brandt's policy to ease tensions, and I hope that every opportunity will be used to improve East and West European relations, including the Warsaw Pact and NATO. The treaty between the Federal Republic of Germany and the Soviet Union, signed in August 1970 by Chancellor Brandt and Chairman Kosygin, is a significant step forward. But it is not to be formally ratified by the German government until progress is made regarding Berlin. Together with the other occupation powers, the British and the French, we should continue to pursue this subject with the Soviets. It would be unfortunate if our differences with them in the Middle East prevented progress in Europe.

For the long run we should not lose sight of the fact that a real detente in Europe requires revision of the Soviet attitude toward its domination of the countries of Eastern Europe. The Soviet Union must learn that a more permanent and sounder security will come from cooperation with the countries of Europe rather than through attempts to dominate its immediate neighbors. Until the Soviet Union abandons its policies as evidenced by the invasion of Czechoslovakia, a firm and united NATO is essential for Western European and our own security.

In Latin America, the Soviets will, I believe, place more emphasis on support of legal Communist parties and their formation of popular fronts than on support for Castro-trained terrorists and guerrillas. The advance of Communism through popular fronts is now being put to the test in Chile. Its advance elsewhere will be significantly affected by whether or not the non-Communist political forces work together and make adequate social progress.

With the early unsuccessful attempts of the Soviets to penetrate Africa, I believe they will limit their activities to special strategic situations such as Somalia, at the entrance to the Red Sea, and to attempt to exploit crises as they did in Nigeria.

Our immediate pressing problem with Russian imperialist expansionism is in the Middle East. This is a dangerous situation, and we should do all we can to encourage a more constructive attitude on the part of Moscow. We should bear in mind that there is usually a division in the Kremlin councils. Some are hard-liners for an aggressive policy and some are more reasonable, more interested in internal developments, and want to see the conflict ended.

At the same time, the Soviets still are continuing to support Communist subversive activities in Latin America. They are helping Castro train young men from a number of countries to be sent back as terrorists and guerrillas to create trouble.

The Latin American countries have generally become more efficient in countering these subversive activities, partly because of our help. President Kennedy did a lot in that field, and Robert Kennedy, as Attorney General, gave it his personal attention. It was worthwhile. Previously, most of our efforts had been to train their armies for conventional warfare. Some of them were just about as capable of dealing with guerrillas as the British Redcoats were fighting the Indians in the eighteenth century. We have also encouraged and helped equip their armies to undertake constructive civic action programs. These have been useful in helping the backward agricultural areas in such things as rural road construction, drainage and small dams for irrigation. We assisted the police in improving their methods of obtaining intelligence on subversive activities and catching the terrorists before they became fully organized. As a result, the Cuban-trained terrorists and guerrillas have been having a rather hard time. But I wish that we could do more to encourage some of the Latin American governments to realize they must make more social progress. The rash of military coups—whether from the right as in Brazil or the left as in Bolivia—is an unfortunate setback. Every effort should be made to induce a return to representative government. To this end we should make more of an effort to mobilize hemisphere-wide public opinion, especially through the OAS.

I am afraid President Nixon's "partnership" as he calls it, is not going to be very effective. I have heard from some of my friends that in Latin America there are not many who are ready to be partners on the basis of President Nixon's statements. Nothing new has been suggested, and, in fact, the old programs have been reduced. In any event, I hope that when the war is over in Vietnam we will take greater leadership in reassuming our share of responsibility for assisting development in Latin America and other parts of the world. In my opinion, this is a *must*.

I am satisfied that there will continue to be a changing scene in Russia. At times greater difficulties will undoubtedly arise, but if we meet them with common sense and sophistication, I believe things will, on balance, improve. Gradually the pressures for individual freedoms within Russia will increase, and in my view the Kremlin will not permanently be able to resist them.

In spite of the present increased restrictions there appears to be a new determination by some intellectuals to resist. There were many letters of protest over the Sinyavsky and Daniel arrests as well as other cases. Intellectuals have been willing to risk punishment to make their views known in the hopes of stirring up domestic and world public opinion that might influence the Kremlin to ease its repressive policies.

Recently, a CBS correspondent brought out from Russia films of interviews with three dissidents which the CBS has broadcast on TV. These men had been imprisoned for their opinions and their writings. They wanted their interviews to be broadcast on television here to inform the American public of the facts regarding their arrests and also to expose the revolting treatment given prisoners in concentration camps and insane asylums. They were ready to risk further persecution in order to have the world know the appalling truth about Soviet repression. These men love their country and don't intend to leave it. They have faith that their sacrifice and that of others will arouse world opinion to such a point that it will induce a change in the present Kremlin benighted attitude and brutal repressive actions against intellectual freedom.

Regardless of immediate results, this shows a new courage and a new determination of many intellectuals to fight for the freedom they fervently believe in. The recent success of protests in securing the release of the eminent Soviet biologist

Dr. Zores Medvedev may be a sign of the future or only an isolated case.

I feel strongly that those of our own intellectuals and students who make excuses for the Communists, overlooking all the abhorrent repression, only set back the cause of these brave men. Also all those who meet Russians at Pugwash or other conferences and contacts should be forceful in denouncing repression even while they encourage, as they should, more contacts and exchange of information and ideas in scientific and aesthetic fields.

In addition, the Soviets will become more and more concerned with their own internal development. There will be less emphasis on Communist expansion, and eventually they will, I think, be willing to do as we are—let the future decide the ideological concepts the world will follow. We believe in freedom for all people in all countries but it is not our principle to try to force other countries to accept our ideas. We should stick to that principle. As soon as we abandon trying to impose President Thieu and his repressive military government on South Vietnam, our voice in the world will be given more credence.

Each agreement we reach with the Soviet Union will help make others easier. That is why I am so unhappy about our present Soviet trade policy. If we would relax trade restrictions today, it would help us in other directions.

I have recently looked over the joint ventures and exchanges that we now have. There are more than people realize—and they go far beyond the track teams and ballet troupes we generally think of. To begin with, exchanges of visits of individuals and groups of scientists, scholars, and others have considerably increased.

Some of the most dramatic proposals—like the idea of our

working together in exploration of outer space—the Russians have turned down. But we are cooperating in Antarctica in some significant activity; scientists from each country spend extended periods of time at the bases of the other. We have an exchange of information on weather and on experiments to try to change the weather. In oceanography there has been a beginning: exchanges of information and in a few cases observers on each other's ships. The Bureau of Mines of the Interior Department has contacts with the Soviets and is undertaking a two-way exchange of coalmining experts this year.

Exchanges are being arranged in which Soviet farmers will study American methods of tomato, cotton, and poultry production, while our scientists will have the chance to study primitive plant forms found only in the Soviet Union. Walker Cisler of Detroit Edison has worked out some very useful exchanges in the public utilities field. The Soviets have been ahead of us in certain aspects of transmission of high voltage electricity over long distances. They have, of course, learned a lot from us over the years in power production.

During the war one of the leading surgeons in our army who came to Moscow told me that in the field of brain surgery the Russians were ahead of us. Of course, the Soviet care of the wounded was in no way comparable to ours. Today, medical exchanges cover a variety of vital fields—among them organ transplants, ophthalmology, heart disease, and cancer research.

Exchanges are even being arranged in areas which used to be regarded as too sensitive, including commercial aircraft and aircraft engine design, and high energy nuclear physics. In fact, a team of American scientists is shortly expected to go to Russia to work with their huge atom smasher, while Soviet scientists are to come here to use an even larger one now under construction in Illinois.

This is all to the good.

There are a number of other ways in which we are moving. I think the Pugwash conferences where scholars and others meet each year are useful. The intimacies established help further understanding on both sides.

However, I think we should have a better understanding than we have about the reaction of Russians to their visits here. There seems to be a popular notion that all we have to do is to invite someone from a Communist country to see our glorious land and they will fall in love with it and with us. This is far from the case. No doubt some do, but many have quite different reactions.

At the United Nations Conference at San Francisco in 1945, the Czech Foreign Minister Jan Masaryk, gave me an interesting insight into Molotov's reaction to what he saw of the United States. He told me that Molotov had insisted that he accompany him on a Sunday drive through the environs of San Francisco. Masaryk said that he himself was much impressed with the beauty of the country and the attractive workmen's homes which showed the widespread economic well-being of the people. Molotov, however, commented, "Think what we could do with this country if we were able to organize it." This showed that the Kremlin leaders were still thinking in the same terms as they had in the twenties— that Communism could best be applied to an industrial society. Molotov was apparently not impressed that a "capitalist" society had achieved these results.

Many Soviets don't understand how we can have such extraordinary opulence along side of poverty and want. The poverty that exists here tends to confirm the Communist doctrine of capitalist exploitation. Although their standard of living is relatively low and a balanced diet by our standards is not generally available in the urban areas, no one in Russia is hungry, and education and medical care are free. Housing is inexpensive, but desperately crowded. Many are still living a family per room.

Some Russian visitors are at times somewhat dismayed by the freedom and disorganization of our life. A recent young visitor complained to an American student that he did not see how one could enjoy a vacation in the United States. In Russia they had two weeks off at a resort and every night was planned for them—a movie one night, a dance the next, and so forth. He complained that he could not understand how anyone could enjoy a vacation in which there was constantly the problem of deciding what to do next.

This story reminded me of a statement that a Russian general made to my daughter Kathleen[10] when we visited Romania in January 1946. He told her that life in Romania seemed to him chaotic, as there was no plan or organization, and each person did what he wanted. On the other hand, one of our Russian-speaking American Embassy staff went to a *kolkhoz* (collective farm) to buy potatoes in the autumn of 1945. He reported that, in his talk with a peasant who had recently been released from the army, the peasant had told him that he had been on the Romanian front. They had been warned not to be taken in by the "fleshpots" of Romanian life. The peasant said, "What did we find? Hard roads to the farms, and what have we got here—mud." He spat on the ground in disgust.

Of course, I believe that the effect of visits by Russians to the United States are on the whole very favorable. However,

[10] The author's daughter, Mrs. Stanley Mortimer, who was with him in Moscow while he served as ambassador.

it is hard to foresee what their reaction will be. I think what seems to impress them the most is if they are welcomed informally by Americans into their homes.

However, we must understand that the Russians continue to be terribly suspicious. During the war they treated us in Moscow in some ways as a potential enemy. For example, as there were no aids to navigation, we used to have a great deal of difficulty in flying in to Moscow with our American plane in bad weather. The Soviets always kindly gave us a Soviet navigator, but his value was similar to that of a guide in the Rocky Mountains. He knew the terrain and as long as he could see the ground he was most helpful.

There were, however, two radio stations in the Moscow region. We knew the location of one and were most anxious to know the location of the other in order to triangulate our position. This they consistently delayed giving us as it was considered a military secret. On one trip we happened to fly over it and so finally knew its location which proved to be most helpful.

Coming into Moscow in bad weather was not easy as the fog sometimes came right down to the treetops. On one occasion we had to fly so low that the pilot had to tip the wings of the plane to avoid church steeples. On another occasion, we were looking for a soft place to land when fortunately the weather lifted sufficiently for us to go on to Moscow just above the treetops. Thanks to the extraordinary skill of our pilot, we never got into trouble.

During the war our military mission in Moscow did exchange intelligence information with the Soviets daily on the enemy order of battle, but they wouldn't give us their own order of battle in any detail because they evidently felt that our security wasn't safe. They saw a lot of military information appearing in our newspapers, and they knew their strict secrecy was an important military asset. For example, the Germans were taken by surprise at Stalingrad because Stalin secretly brought up several of his Siberian divisions and attacked on the northern flank and thus broke the siege. Hitler was taken by surprise in other actions. The Soviet suspicion of us made us quite angry at the start, until we began to understand their concerns. Then I had a certain amount of sympathy for it. I, too, was quite upset to find that some of the information we sent to Washington got into our press. It is very hard for us to stop all leaks. The Soviets have the power to do it.

During the war I knew quite well some of the intellectuals. Among them was Alexis Tolstoy a distant relative of the famous Leo Tolstoy. Alexis also wrote historical novels. He grew up under the czarist regime and had gone to Paris during the Revolution. But he came back. He loved Russia and wanted to live in his homeland, so he conformed to the rules and wrote about things that were "appropriate." He explained that up to the war the history of the Soviet Union began with the October Revolution in 1917, but that in order to arouse patriotism among all the people during the war, Stalin ordered the rewriting of Soviet history to interpret the Revolution as a part of the mainstream of Russian tradition. The old Czars, even Ivan the Terrible, became the protectors of the people's interest, against the exploitation of the boyars. Czarist generals such as Suvorov and Kutuzov were revived as great heroes and defenders of Mother Russia.

Tolstoy told me a great deal about Russia and the Kremlin. One of the things he said was that to understand the Kremlin today, one had to understand the Kremlin of Ivan the Terrible and Peter the Great. He meant that the Soviet system was Communism superimposed on Old Russia and Russian customs.

Tolstoy pointed out that it was hard for Americans to understand Russians—their backgrounds and emotions were so different. He told me the story of a peasant who had put up a traveler for the night. The peasant had shared with his guest his loaf of bread and his last bottle of vodka, and they got drunk together. The next morning the peasant woke up first. He thought he had been taken in and so he cut the traveler's throat and took his money. Tolstoy told me this story to illustrate the volatile temperament of Russian character but also to show the Russian peasants' suspicion of any stranger, not only foreigners.

Some of the things the Soviets do now are inherited, among them is their suspicion of foreigners. It will take some time for them to be freer and easier. However, most of the Russian people have a longing to know what is going on abroad and would like to have contacts with foreigners, particularly Americans. Yet the government fears it will give their people "bad ideas" and interfere with its plans to control the Soviet mind.

So it is going to be a long, slow pull. We will have to have a lot of patience and we must take the initiatives to break down the resistances. I can't emphasize that too much. What disturbs me is the tendency in this Administration to treat the Russians with over-suspicion—or at least the wrong kind of suspicion. Unless we make the gestures, unless we move at least halfway to meet them, very little progress will be made. Of course, in negotiations that is another matter. There we have to be firm and determined on our objectives. We have to be firm and determined, too, in the United Nations and elsewhere in opposing positions that they take that are contrary to our principles and our interests. In 1946 when I returned from being Ambassador in Moscow, I said publicly that in dealing with the Soviets our guard must be up but at the same time we should always hold out a friendly hand. Although the situation has changed, the same principle holds true today.

In early March, 1946, shortly after my return I had a radio interview with Quentin Reynolds. I quote it to show my attitude at that time. I could say much the same today.

> **Reynolds:** Mr. Harriman, do you believe that war with Russia is inevitable?
>
> **Harriman:** I most certainly do not. But it depends principally on us.
>
> **Reynolds:** What do you mean by that?
>
> **Harriman:** Well, what I am going to say may not sound very down-to-earth, but actually it is. There will be no war if we, as a country, remain strong, physically and spiritually. By physical strength I am not speaking only of the maintenance of an adequate military establishment, important as that is, I mean that we must maintain a healthy economic life—an expanding life for all of our people. Through our system of individual initiative we did a fantastic war production job. You remember that at Teheran Stalin told us that American industrial production was making the defeat of Hitler possible. This was accomplished by the genius and initiative of American management in big business and small and by the intelligence and vigor of the men

and women who worked in the war plants and on the farms as well. In this combination lies the real physical strength of America—a combination that must be just as effective in the future to work for our objectives in peace as it has in war.

Reynolds: What do you mean by staying spiritually strong?

Harriman: The ideals which we hold in America give hope to most of the people of the world. If we are to retain this moral leadership we must guard these ideals of ours; we must protect them.

Reynolds: When you talk of the American ideals, do you mean the freedom we enjoy?

Harriman: Yes, that's just it. But of all these freedoms, I think that President Roosevelt's conception of freedom from want comes first. Man can't attain other freedoms if he is hungry.

Our first job is to see that there's no want in our country. That certainly we can do. But, in other parts of the world where I've been, I've seen hungry people. They have nowhere to look but to the United States. No one realizes this more than President Truman. He has asked Herbert Hoover to join him in putting this problem before the American people.

Reynolds: Many people are saying that the Russian ideology is so different from our own that it will prevent permanent peace between us. What about that?

Harriman: It is a fact that the Russian ideology is completely different from ours, but if we both adopt the attitude of live and let live, as to internal affairs, and if we both respect the right of all people to choose their own way of life, this barrier needn't be insurmountable. Most of the people of the world know that this is the attitude of the United States and are counting on us to stand firm against any nation that won't abide by this principle. This may lead to differences of opinion in the months to come; it may lead to situations difficult to deal with, but, as long as we as a nation stand firm by our principles, I have faith that these principles will prevail. When I said that we must remain spiritually strong, that's what I meant. As long as we're true to our principles and ready to back them up, I cannot believe that there will be war.

Reynolds: Now, it seems to me that the Russian policy has been, to put it mildly, uncooperative during the past few months. I think that millions of Americans feel that way too. What's your opinion?

Harriman: I agree with you. Since the war, the Soviet policy has been difficult to deal with. Today Russia wants security.

Reynolds: And goodness knows she is entitled to security.

Harriman: But, actually, she seems inclined to get this security by insisting upon dominating her neighbors. We ourselves have only recently learned that to have really friendly neighbors a big country must first show tolerance and understanding toward a small country. A nation with newly found strength is apt to throw its weight around.

Reynolds: Do you think that Russia can be induced to change its point of view?

Harriman: That's a tough one. We agree that Russia is entitled to security. She suffered horribly during the war. You and I were in Stalingrad and

Smolensk and dozens of other cities completely devastated. But, in gaining this security I still hope that Russia will accept, as we have, that the chief hope of the world is in collective security through the United Nations. Any country which attempts to gain security through unilateral action, through aggressive independent action, is only opening the gates of disaster. I believe that if we maintain confidence in the United Nations and take a firm stand with any nation that attempts to take unilateral action which infringes upon the freedom of other nations, there will not be another war. But I always come back to the point that above all, we in America must retain our physical and spiritual strength in order to give the world the moral leadership that it is looking for.

Reynolds: You've only been back a couple of weeks, but I think you'll find that a great many Americans think that the spread of Communism will be a threat to our way of life. Do you agree with them?

Harriman: I feel it is a challenge rather than a threat; that is, if we have faith in our way of life. Throughout the centuries, men have fought for freedom. We Americans have inherited that freedom. We believe that a society of free men is the highest form of civilization, and we believe that we have that and are constantly developing it so that all of our people can get the full benefits. No nation has ever done the job we have under our form of government either in peace or in war. And remember that during the war we retained our freedom. That was the greatest test of all. We maintained a free press, and we held free elections. I suppose that the more you live abroad, the more you appreciate

America, the more faith you have in America. I can't believe that Communism can be a real threat to our way of living. [End of interview.]

Confrontations with the Soviet Union will continue to occur in various situations and in different parts of the world. I believe if we face these carefully and with understanding, we can find ways to work out settlements one by one. Of all the situations that have arisen in the postwar period, the manner in which President Kennedy handled the Cuban missile crisis in 1962 was perhaps the most successful. I believe President Kennedy's decisions are a classic example of wise action in achieving a satisfactory conclusion of an extremely dangerous threat. The principles he adhered to should be guidelines to any President or in fact any head of government in dealing with a crisis. They are applicable today in dealing with the Soviet Union and other situations.

First and foremost President Kennedy tried to look at things as they appeared to Chairman Khrushchev. He tried to avoid saying publicly or doing anything unnecessarily provocative which would make it more difficult for Khrushchev to remove the offensive missiles from Cuba.

After establishing the naval "quarantine," he directed action in every detail. He let a Soviet tanker and an East German passenger ship go through and then boarded not a Soviet ship but a Panamanian-owned ship of Lebanese registry under Soviet charter, which it was found was not carrying any military cargo. He wanted to show firmness in the least provocative way. At the time the Navy protested vigorously, maintaining that it was their responsibility to make these decisions, but this protest did not deter him.

The dramatic account of these events is recorded in Robert Kennedy's *Thirteen Days*, published posthumously. President Kennedy disregarded proposals from the military and others for air strikes on the missile sites or the invasion of Cuba. This is not a reflection on the competence of our military leaders but it underlines that in dealing with a political objective the military point of view must frequently be set aside. Our Chiefs of Staff must give their advice from a military standpoint, and it is not within their responsibility or competence to weigh political against military considerations. In a crisis, political considerations should be given first attention since the avoidance of war is of prime importance, and President Kennedy knew that was *his* responsibility.

An effective procedure he followed was to insist that his advisers meet without him. He recognized that it was difficult for men to argue out their differences or to take sharp issue with cabinet members or senior military officers in front of a President. On the other hand, men meeting alone can thrash out their differences fully and frankly and can more readily reach a consensus opinion. At least the nature of the disagreements can then be more precisely presented to the President. I think the President learned this from the inadequacy of discussion among his advisers leading to the Bay of Pigs blunder.

President Kennedy wanted to be sure to avoid misunderstandings and miscalculations that have caused wars in the past and therefore established an intimate channel of communication between himself and Khrushchev: his brother Robert Kennedy talked with the Soviet Ambassador Dobrynin frequently. The President knew that word coming through that channel would carry more weight and meaning than a more formal State Department communication.

One of Kennedy's most striking decisions was his selection of the best in Khrushchev's messages, not the worst. People are apt to look at the worst that an opponent says, and this digs a deeper disagreement. Kennedy chose to disregard the latest, intransigent message he received from Khrushchev and go back to the preceding one. He selected points he could accept and built an agreement on them.

Of vital importance was that he took the time at some risk to seek world-wide understanding and support of our position. He consulted and obtained the unanimous approval of our Latin American neighbors, the members of the OAS. He informed other allies as well. He also had Ambassador Adlai Stevenson bring our case to the United Nations Security Council with irrefutable air-photographic evidence of the missile sites.

As a result, the Soviet missiles were removed and the dangerous threat eliminated without firing a shot.

Success in negotiation requires efforts to understand the other country's objectives and a willingness to accept those we can without giving away anything important. We must not be rigid on the way to reach our goals. We should be very firm on our vital goals but flexible on the road that gets there. If one can find common ground on some point it is generally less difficult to compose remaining differences. We can be tough in private and not hesitate to state publicly the facts as we see them, but we should not be needlessly provocative in public statements.

The Soviets have wanted to see us end the war in Vietnam. Kosygin in 1965 gave me a rough going-over about the war. He maintained that it only helped Peking, and made it difficult for them to reach bilateral agreements with us on nuclear and other questions. He urged a political settlement in Vietnam. It seems clear that they want to see Southeast Asia strong enough and independent enough to check Chinese advance to the south. They will never come to an agreement with an "imperialist-capitalist country," as they like to call us, against another Communist country, but we can find ourselves in parallel positions, as we have in India and Pakistan. Both of us help both of them. I think the same thing can be developed in Southeast Asia—not with the idea of ganging up offensively against China. I think that would be a mistake. But simply, we would both oppose Chinese expansion into their neighbors to the south. So in many ways and situations, "parallelism" is an applicable term and is quite correct.

An over-all detente is not now possible. The will to extend Communism is still too strong, and Russian traditional expansionism, as in the Middle East, is a driving force. *Competitive* coexistence will continue. We must accept and meet that challenge.

Bilaterally, we can come, as I have said, to specific understandings. I am not unoptimistic—to use the British double negative—about the developments of our relations, step by step, if we will be ourselves in what we do. We must remain strong, firm in our principles and yet an outgoing, understanding people whose prime objective is to seek peace in the world.

The objective of peace cannot be furthered by a passive approach or by a neo-isolationist outlook. Vigorous, purposeful action must be taken.

It is a popular cliche these days to say we must not be the world policeman. That has never been the policy of any administration I have worked for, although some enthusiastic or terrified anti-Communists would get us overextended. We should learn from Vietnam to judge carefully our national interests and the limits of our capabilities. We should exercise the greatest care to avoid involving United States military forces.

On the other hand, this is a small planet and getting smaller all the time. We can be affected by what goes on almost anywhere. This requires that our government keep well informed and, if appropriate, take sensible and limited steps when a situation is of real concern to us. This might be some suitable assistance or the raising of the issue in the United Nations or a regional organization.

The United Nations must have our continued, in fact increased, understanding and support. With the deep division among the great powers, the Security Council has not been able to play as decisive a role as had been hoped. It has assisted, however, directly or indirectly in a considerable number of situations over the years, and we should exert our influence to expand this role by our example and in other ways. We were right in Korea where we got United Nations participation. We took a wrong turn in Vietnam when we went it largely alone, and it is now tragic to continue on that course. Now again we have been wise to use the UN to the fullest extent possible in the dangerous Middle East conflict.

Regional organizations contemplated by the United Nations Charter, like the OAS, can contribute substantially to peaceful settlements. The fact that President Kennedy obtained the unanimous support of the OAS members during the Cuban missile crisis contributed significantly to its successful conclusion.

The United Nations has had outstanding achievements through some of its affiliates and has done effective work through the others—the World Health Organization, the Food and Agriculture Organization, the World Bank, the International Monetary Fund, the UN Development Program, and the UN Children's Fund (UNICEF)—to mention some.

The United Nations and its affiliates can play an increasing useful part in coping with growing planetary problems such as environment, population growth, and ocean resources. All these activities should have our strong support and imaginative guidance.

We should not be ashamed of our virtues. We should not underestimate the extraordinary vitality of our ideals and fine traditions. I have very little patience with those young people of today who think that everything before them was wrong. I don't blame them for being concerned about Vietnam; I am too. But I have very little patience for those who do not recognize our enormous heritage. This country has symbolized man's highest hopes and principles. It has achieved the greatest production the world has ever seen. Use all this well. Learn from past mistakes and try to improve on the past. I don't mean to lecture, but I am utterly impatient with some who talk about overthrowing this whole nation. Put it in the right path, make America live up to her highest principles, even improve the traditions if you will. But don't decry the past. Understand the past. Build on it for a better America. My guess is you will.

★ ★ ★

Q   Are we finished in Paris?

WAH   No, we haven't begun. I don't want to be abrupt.
        The North Vietnamese sent Le Duc Tho to Paris. He
        is one of their seniors. I talked with him many times
        and he spoke with authority. He is a member of
        their politburo, one of the top half dozen men in
        Hanoi. They sent him to Paris to negotiate. It's the
        proper place to negotiate. We can get negotiation
        going in Paris if President Thieu will field a team
        from South Vietnam that wants to negotiate—not
        Thieu himself because he has made it plain he
        doesn't want to negotiate. And we must send a man
        of responsibility and position to take Lodge's place.[11]
        There's no need to have a new negotiation started
        elsewhere. It's well situated where it is. Eventually
        we might want to bring in other interested countries
        to adhere to an agreement, to associate themselves
        with it. That was done before, in 1954 and 1962.
        It might be well to get both Russia and China, as
        well as France and Britain, and the other countries
        of Southeast Asia to go along with any agreement.
        But the fundamental agreement must be made be-
        tween the four that are now in Paris—the North
        Vietnamese and the NLF, the South Vietnamese
        and the United States.

Q   Governor Harriman, there has been a lot of hoopla
        about President Nixon's withdrawal of troops. I was
        wondering if you have the actual figures of men re-
        moved and not replaced by the normal new men
        brought in.

[11] Statement made prior to the appointment of Ambassador David K. E.
Bruce to this post in July 1970 and subsequent events.

WAH   I am sure the figures announced are entirely correct. There isn't any doubt but that our military give out those figures accurately. One hundred and ten thousand will have been withdrawn by the middle of April 1970.

The President has stated that one hundred and fifty thousand more will be withdrawn by the spring of 1971. That means that after two and one half years in office less than half our men will have been withdrawn—and no indication whether or when the balance of our forces will be withdrawn.

Q   There has been recent talk about the world tending toward a division into "have" and "have not" countries. Is this difference accentuating, and will it eventually lead to mass starvation in the "have not" countries?

WAH   I think it is fairly clear that with the improved methods of agricultural production, it would be possible to avoid it. That is if the underdeveloped countries take advantage of these improvements. That will require a lot of investment in terms of fertilizer plants, irrigation, roads, development of markets. In addition, individual farmers must be trained and governments must adopt adequate land tenure policies. Also there must be balanced economic growth to give jobs and income for people to buy food.

The industrial countries during the past two decades have been able to expand extraordinarily. There was a miracle in Japan, in Germany, and in northern Italy as well. It is hard to remember that twenty years ago in the Marshall Plan days when some of the best economists in Europe were planning the future, it was estimated that in order to be viable, in order to eliminate unemployment, Italy would have to permanently export about five hundred thousand citizens a year. The idea that there should be a labor shortage in northern Italy—as there is today—if anyone had suggested it at that time they would have been thought crazy. There has been an extraordinary rate of development of the industrialized countries. But it has been very much more difficult to get the rate of growth in the underdeveloped countries to catch up. Therefore, unfortunately, the gap between the developing nations and the industrialized nations is growing every year, and we ought to give a good deal more thought and attention to this. We have got to view development also from the standpoint of our own well-being. In the first place, whenever countries develop, our business with them grows and it helps us. But also we should not be ashamed of helping because it is the right thing to do. This idea of coldly leaving them to their own fate doesn't appeal to me as being either wise in judgment or sympathetic in heart.

But on this question of hunger, I think we can avoid starvation if we work together, and if these plans for population control are implemented. They are moving, but moving very slowly. Still they are taking hold, and there is an understanding in the world as never before of the necessity of reducing population growth.

Q   You have mentioned something about Chinese expansionism and certain countries like India and

Pakistan which are being utilized to check this expansion southward. Would you please amplify the statement?

WAH   Speaking of China's expansion south, in India both we and the Russians have been helping the Indians to strengthen themselves economically and to some extent militarily, now particularly the Russians. It's up to India to defend itself. We have never had any plans to come to India's aid with American forces. I don't see why we should. But it is to our interest, I think, to help India maintain its independence, achieve its own objective of being able to defend itself.

When India was attacked by Red China in October 1962 President Kennedy sent me to India with a military mission to find out India's needs. We, together with the British, did supply her with military equipment to help in her defense. We also attempted at that time to reconcile the differences between India and Pakistan, particularly over Kashmir, to assure that the military equipment we were giving both countries would not be used against each other rather than for common defense. Later when hostilities did break out between them in 1965, the Soviet Union undertook to mediate a settlement. The fighting was stopped but no agreement on Kashmir was reached.

Q   What about the continued presence of American troops in South Korea?

WAH   We have forces there, but the main defense is now by the South Koreans themselves. They have recently had an extraordinary development for an underdeveloped country. We were ready to take some of our troops out before the South Koreans sent troops to Vietnam, but we wanted to keep a reserve in the area and we didn't have any other place to put them. I don't think we have any reason to regret what was done in Korea. We helped the South Koreans defend themselves from the open invasion that came from the north. It was done by vote under the direction of the United Nations. The South Korean nation is beginning to stand on its own feet. It is not an industrial nation and needs military equipment from us, but it is not dependent on our troops at the present time, unless there was a major invasion supported by Chinese forces. Of course, the presence of some American troops is a deterrent to another reckless attack.

Q   Governor Harriman, concerning Korea. In January 1968, before the Tet offensive, the *Pueblo* was taken into captivity for a year. During August of that year, President Nixon, accepting the nomination for the Republican Party for President, stated, "When I am President, no fourth-rate power will seize one of our ships on the high seas." That March of his Administration in 1969 one of our U.S. planes was shot down. Would you be able to amplify the tactics or the alternatives under the Johnson administration and under the Nixon administration?

WAH   I think you ought to address your question to Mr. Nixon.

But one thing I would like to add. There is little worse than trying to arouse American chauvinism. I must say that I don't like the reports one hears of Mr. Agnew going around slurring the patriotism and character of young people who want the war ended. He calls them by different names and says he'd trade the whole bunch of them for one platoon of soldiers fighting in Vietnam. The audience rose and cheered. Now, I don't think that's a cheer that is worth getting.

Q   Is the domino theory really applicable to the Southeast Asia situation?

WAH   Well, I don't know what the domino theory really means. There is no doubt that the people in the general area, like Lee Kuan Yew in Singapore, are very anxious to see the expansion of Communism checked, and just what influence it would have on his country if another country should go Communist I can't say. I know very little about the North Vietnamese, but one thing I know is that they are fiercely nationalistic, and they want to be independent of Peking. I would hope the South Vietnamese— the majority of them—want to be independent and establish non-Communist government of their own. They won't succeed under Thieu, but I think they could if we would encourage the formation of an alliance of the non-Communist forces. But if they should decide to adopt Communism, I don't know that it would make much difference to other countries, providing they were to live with their neighbors in peace—leave Laos alone, Cambodia and Thailand alone. It's the attitude they would take that is important. Tito, for example, is not a threat to the peace and security of his neighbors.

This domino theory presupposes, I imagine, that a monolithic structure of international Communism still exists. But that has been shattered. Not only is there the basic struggle between Peking and

Moscow, but Tito has defected, and the Communist parties of other countries take a much more independent line. Both the French and Italian Communist Parties publicly opposed the Soviet's occupation of Czechoslovakia. You see the hold that Moscow used to have is broken, the Communist international movement is no longer a monolithic structure. So I am skeptical of generalizations about dominoes.

Q   Are there any realistic prospects in present steps toward disarmament?

WAH   Well, I can say there have been. The limited test ban agreement was a step in the right direction. There have been several other important agreements in the nuclear field since that, and I am hopeful that an even more important one can be reached in the SALT talks. One of the things that Kosygin mentioned to me in 1965 as a step to be taken was the mutual reduction in military budgets. Talks along these lines were going on before the Vietnamese war heated up. I think that if we can get rid of that war, this would be a useful subject to discuss. It is true we don't know fully what their budgets are, but we do have sufficient information to justify an understanding in this field.

There are other ways in which we can make progress in disarmament. Among them are discussions between NATO and Warsaw—a European security conference. And the first subject of discussion should be the mutual balanced reduction in the level of forces.

General disarmament, complete disarmament, I think is a long way off. But step-by-step, controlled limitation of armaments in different regions and reduction of forces facing each other can be achieved. Of course, the two important factors are the United States and the Soviet Union, and I want to say again that we have to be willing to take the initiative.

Q   Governor Harriman, since returning from the Paris negotiations, you have been very critical of the United States negotiating position and particularly of the Thieu-Ky regimes' negotiating position. Now, I am sure you must have, at least to some degree, held these views when you were in Paris. Weren't there things that you could have done by means of the press or other subtle techniques by which you could have brought pressure to bear on President Johnson and likewise on the Saigon regime and thereby weakened the negotiating position of the South Vietnamese government?

WAH   You have never worked for President Johnson. You couldn't use the press against him because if you tried, you would be fired that same day. There was a difference of opinion among his advisers, as has been written, between those who wanted to bring about negotiations for peaceful settlement, and those who looked more toward continued military pressure.

You know, this talk about winning wars of limited objective does not make sense. At times military force is used to achieve a political objective. You are not trying to win a total military victory—only achieve your political objectives. People don't seem to understand that you don't "win" a limited war.

As far as Paris is concerned, of course Thieu

blocked progress in the negotiations. He ran out
on President Johnson when he refused to join the
negotiations in Paris in early November as he had
agreed to. Later he stalled over the shape of the
table until the Nixon administration came in in January.

Q   What effect will the present effort of the new
regime in Germany to court the East have on
America-Soviet relations?

WAH   Well, I think Willy Brandt's objectives are very
helpful. I talked at length with both Kosygin and
Khrushchev about Germany. The Russians have a
very ingrown fear of Germany. Stalin had it; Molotov
had it. The Germans through history have been more
efficient than the Russians. They have been concerned about the Germans even after they, themselves, had the superiority of nuclear weapons. I
don't think they are now afraid of the Germans so
much as they are afraid that Germany will get us into
a conflict because we would join the German side. I
think that is a real concern to the Russians. They
don't want another war. It's wrong for our Secretary of Defense to state publicly that he has special
intelligence information that the Kremlin is planning a first strike. There's no such information, and
Secretary of State Rogers denied it. We do have to
look at their capabilities, however, and they are
expanding their capabilities to a point where they
have more land-based inter-continental ballistic missiles than we have, but their over-all nuclear capability is still less than ours. However, the overriding
consideration is that both of us have sufficient capa-

bility that an attack on the other side would be an act of national suicide.

Q   What do you think of the possibility of war between Russia and China?

WAH   I talked a little bit about Stalin's un-relationships with Mao Tse-tung—"a margarine Communist" as Stalin called him. There was never much good will between Moscow and Peking. They patched up their difficulties for a while. In 1959 the trouble seemed to begin, and in 1960 the Russians took out their advisers and stopped sending industrial equipment. That created a lot of bitterness both ways. Now, what will happen in the future between China and Moscow I don't think anybody knows. I certainly don't. It's conceivable when there are changes in personalities in China—new leadership— they would be willing to patch up their differences. But it's not in the cards now because there isn't any new leadership in sight that would do it. Moreover, there has been deep-seated feeling historically between the Russians and the Chinese. The Chinese are very unpopular—you know if you've been to Moscow—among the Russian people themselves. So they are probably in for a long pull.

Now, our policy should be to be ourselves with each of them—not attempt in any way to use the conflict to our advantage. There are a number of reasons for that. In the first place, I don't think we are devious enough to know how to do it. Perhaps that's enough of a reason. In the second place, it would be counter-productive to try to do it.

We should try to improve our relations with Peking and I've got to say that I do approve some

things that have been done. I am not always critical.
I think that moves which have been made to try
to improve our relations with China are good, such
as the offer of the exchange of visitors and some
indirect trade. They don't go far enough, but they
are a good step forward.

Q   I remember your telling a story once about an incident when you were Ambassador in Moscow. You got a note from the Russians and rejected it right on the spot, then later notified the State Department of what you had done. Now modern communications have changed things, and the whole theme of diplomacy these days seems to be, "Check with Washington before you move." Do you think this is a good thing, or do you think it's hurt diplomacy generally?

WAH   The case you speak of was the surrender terms for Japan. Stalin proposed that a Soviet commander, as well as General MacArthur, accept the Japanese surrender together. We had to answer right away. I rejected this in the name of my government, and, as I was informing Washington that night, Stalin withdrew the demand. But that was a special case.

[I had believed that Stalin had in mind claiming a Soviet zone of occupation in Japan—as they had in Germany—the northern island of Hokkaido. This claim would have been enhanced if we permitted a Red Army general to join with General MacArthur in accepting the surrender of Japan, and I was determined to block it.]

The speed in communications has changed the job of an ambassador or a negotiator. I'm amused to read accounts of the Congress of Vienna . . . in 1815—the positions each one of these negotiators took, the length of time, the months it took for a British negotiator to get an answer back from London and the amount of authority that these people assumed in committing their governments. The personalities of the negotiators were fascinating. Some had more courage than others. But with communications that difficult, a government had to have a negotiator in whom they had complete confidence.

Now, it is quite different. But still a negotiator is of very great importance because opportunities arise, he has to see them rapidly, he has to report accurately, his recommendations are important. He gets a "feel" from the talk with people. The surest way not to come to any agreement is to send carefully worded legalistic notes back and forth. Initiative and recommendation and the sense of feel are as essential today as ever.[12]

[12] Extracted from "Harriman Suggests a Way Out of Vietnam," by Hedrick Smith, the New York *Times Magazine*, August 24, 1969. Used with permission.